GW00854574

Girl in the
MIRROR

JEAN BERRY

BALBOA.
PRESS

A DIVISION OF HAY HOUSE

Copyright © 2013 Jean Berry.

All rights reserved. No part of this book may be used or reproduced by any means, graphic, electronic, or mechanical, including photocopying, recording, taping or by any information storage retrieval system without the written permission of the publisher except in the case of brief quotations embodied in critical articles and reviews.

This book is a work of non-fiction based on the experiences, recollections and reflections of the author. In all cases, the names of people, places and some detail of events have been changed to protect the privacy of others. Every effort has been made to maintain the authenticity of the story.

Balboa Press books may be ordered through booksellers or by contacting:

Balboa Press
A Division of Hay House
1663 Liberty Drive
Bloomington, IN 47403
www.balboapress.com
1 (877) 407-4847

Because of the dynamic nature of the Internet, any web addresses or links contained in this book may have changed since publication and may no longer be valid. The views expressed in this work are solely those of the author and do not necessarily reflect the views of the publisher, and the publisher hereby disclaims any responsibility for them.

The author of this book does not dispense medical advice or prescribe the use of any technique as a form of treatment for physical, emotional, or medical problems without the advice of a physician, either directly or indirectly. The intent of the author is only to offer information of a general nature to help you in your quest for emotional and spiritual well-being. In the event you use any of the information in this book for yourself, which is your constitutional right, the author and the publisher assume no responsibility for your actions.

Any people depicted in stock imagery provided by Thinkstock are models, and such images are being used for illustrative purposes only.
Certain stock imagery © Thinkstock.

Printed in the United States of America.

ISBN: 978-1-4525-8811-7 (sc)
ISBN: 978-1-4525-8813-1 (hc)
ISBN: 978-1-4525-8812-4 (e)

Library of Congress Control Number: 2013922190

Balboa Press rev. date: 5/21/2014

CONTENTS

We may not realize it now, but we treat our children abominably. Children of the future will look back to children of the present in their history classes and will cry.

Lorna Byrne
Stairways to Heaven

This story is dedicated to the one, in my family, who always looked lost. May this book find him, and may he know that we were all lost too.

To my leading man, Pierce; thank you for your love.

To Kay, my reiki healer and teacher: thank you for guiding me back towards neutral.

To the Balboa Press team; thank you for your professional and insightful support. You are a fantastic team.

Only from the point of neutrality—the whole truth—can we know the difference between right and wrong, positive and negative.

This can help bring us together or push us poles apart.

This is our choice.

*   *   *

I have stripped myself bare for good reason.
This is my choice.

I have the right to stand up to those who
have silenced me for too long.
This is my choice.

I have the right for the whole truth to be known.
This is my choice.

We feed our minds daily with knowledge, yet let us not forget to feed our spirits daily with truth.

Introduction: Why

March 2012

I am writing this book to help in the way others have helped me—with kind, heartfelt, loving advice. It is my hope that children of alcoholics and abuse victims like me will see that they are not alone; I hope to encourage them to reach out for help in whatever way they can.

I am writing to explain what happened to me, to explain my now-changing self. I do this so I will never forget, so I will never change back.

I am writing to explain that in my world, for a very long time everything appeared normal (or healthy even). Everyone else may have thought I was normal too, except those who cared to look deeply into my eyes. They would ask, "Are you okay?" Those who cared to keep on looking would see an agony so terribly deep that they didn't know where to start.

They would try to help. I would cry simple tears in reply—not too many, but they were deep. I was afraid to let them out. I was afraid they would never stop. I didn't know what was wrong with me, so how could I tell them? I didn't know why I was crying. I couldn't understand it. "Try to get some counseling," they would gently say. I would say, "Maybe," but never would.

Eventually they would stop trying, and I would move on. I was out of reach; I was untouchable. I was in denial, mostly to myself. I was in so deep, and I couldn't see a way out. I didn't know where to go. I had nowhere to go—until now.

I was one tragedy leading to the next like a major car crash waiting to happen. From afar you can see everything clearly, but when you're in it you don't see that one bad choice, one poor decision on your part or someone else's, leads to an unavoidable collision. That was me. Along the way I banged into everyone and everything but just kept going on the same road—until now.

I see now that I am the only person who can put a halt to these endless collisions. I see that I am the driver of this car—that I am the one in control. It's me, just me. There is no one to cling to and no one to throw tantrums at anymore. They are all gone. They are too tired to listen.

Here's where I am. I stopped my car. I pulled over to the side of the curb three months ago. I stopped everything to look back—really look back. No peeping through the mirror, no quick flick around and back again. I stopped, and the whole world stopped too, at least for me.

For the first time in my life, I am stationary.

Surprisingly enough, I am still here in exactly the same location. I didn't think I would be able to remain here. My family, who are exhausted, are still here too; they are waiting for me to calm down. They are waiting for everything to go back to the way it was.

But that isn't going to happen. I'm not going back. I'm only going forward, and to do that, I have had to strip myself bare. In doing so, I know I am making myself whole once more from the inside out.

As I look back, unfortunately it's the traumatic events that dominate my memories; the good ones seem to be blocked out. Perhaps I can't remember them because the bad ones have such a profound effect on me. They are what nightmares are made of. They are haunting dreams that never go away. I feel faint just thinking of them. In fact, I feel faint quite a lot. My stomach churns and churns, leaving a vacant emptiness behind. It drains my energy, and my heart is heavy. These are the telling signs.

I look gaunt and tired from exhaustion. I am worn out. I am thirty-eight years old, but inside I harbor a seven-year-old's plight.

My body aches from a deep hurt that permeates me deep inside. It's everywhere, but mostly it's in my heart. It is hardly beating. It is lifeless. It wants to give up; it wants out of all its misery. It wants to die.

* * *

This book is not about blame. Rather it is about taking responsibility for one's actions, and this can only be done through awareness—awareness around the things we do to each other and how we come to a conclusion that these things are somehow acceptable just because they are not intentional. It's also about taking responsibility for our own happiness, and that is what I am doing. Telling the truth makes me happy. It has taken the heavy load off my weary shoulders.

This book has been written with love—lots of it. I hope someday all will see that. I am doing this to help all those who are close to me understand. I am doing this to give answers, especially the unasked ones. I am doing this to reach out in the only way I can.

I am doing this to help all accept the new me, for there is no going back; what I accepted then I would never accept again. I am forever changed for the better.

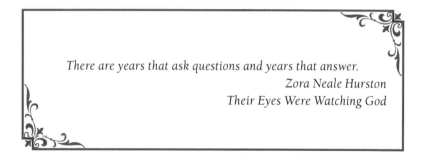

There are years that ask questions and years that answer.
Zora Neale Hurston
Their Eyes Were Watching God

CHAPTER 1

Where My Questions Begin— My Mum and Dad

1978

*M*y earliest memory as a child is at our big front doors. They are mahogany, glossed to the nines and beautiful. They are big, heavy, expansive double doors. I see them clearly as if I am there right now.

I am on the wrong side of them. They are closed, slammed shut as if in a hurry. My mum and dad are scurrying away on the other side like two little mice. I can hear their every move. They never told me they were leaving. I just happen to be going past the door when I hear a noise. It is accidental. I am not supposed to hear them. I am not supposed to know.

I am furious! How dare they? Where are they going without me? There is no one else in the house but me, a little four-year-old. I reach for the nearest thing to pull me up. It is the gold umbrella stand; it's full of all kinds of umbrellas. I roll it over toward the middle of the two doors and clamber up on it as quickly as possible to get to the bolt on top.

I unlock the door as speedily as my little hands let me. I am good at things like this. I love adventure; no place is hidden from me. But now I am in a hurry. I am panicking. I am being left behind. I just know it. It feels like I am about to lose something—something very special—and it is not coming back; it is never coming back. I run out and scream "Mammy, Mammy. Where are you going?" I cry wildly.

In my hand is a big, black umbrella I happened to pick up along the way. I don't know how or why. I begin to hit my mother with it from behind. She is still walking away following Dad. He, my dad, is not even bothering to look back; she, fleetingly so. If she hurries she can make it to the car before I catch her. How dare she? How dare she do this to me? I get closer. I'm faster than her. I'm more determined than her. I get up close and hit her hard. She has no choice but to stop now. She has no choice.

She says little by way of reply. She just stops and looks at me. I can see that she is annoyed. She is annoyed with me. I am in her way. Dad continues to the car as if nothing has happened. He just ignores my pleas. He gets into the car. He is ready to go. I hear the engine coming on.

She does nothing for a moment, a very long moment. She says nothing. She always says nothing. I can see now that she is panicking just like I was a minute ago. I recognize that panicky feeling, the same one as mine. Hers takes over mine. I stop and stand back to look up at her as if from afar. I am in shock. I can't believe this is happening to me.

She moves in fast, still nothing, not a word. I'm shaking with pain. Every core of my body just wishes that she would hug me and tell me that everything is going to be okay. Surely it's going to be okay now that she sees my pain? But it's not okay. Nothing will ever be okay again; something deep inside tells me so.

She doesn't hug me. Instead she bends down and quietly, deliberately tears the umbrella from my little hands. Coldly she picks me up. She puts me firmly back inside the door. It's decisive;

there is no feeling here. She doesn't see my tears. She doesn't see my fear. She doesn't see my pain. She only sees Dad.

She only hears the engine purring in the background signaling that it's time to go, before he changes his mind and leaves without her too. She closes the heavy doors in front of me. I sob and sob until finally I can sob no more. I stop. It's quiet, eerily quiet. I get up resigned to the fact that I have been forgotten. I decide to forget about them too for a while. I begin to play. I know deep inside that this is the best thing to do. I know that they're not coming back anytime soon. I know that I am irrelevant.

*   *   *

I was born into a family of seven. We lived in a vast seven-bedroom house with an indoor swimming pool and lots of garages in a small town in North Cork in southern Ireland. The gardens were lavish. I was the baby of the family. My dad would tell anyone who cared to hear that they saved the best till last. His voice would boom with gusts of laughter once these very words were uttered. He also told of how I was the only one to be born in hospital to a doctor of another color and creed. I was born in 1974, five years after the sixth child. Somehow this gap was to be the beginning of a new generation while the rest remained part of the old.

It was unusual at the time to either be born in a hospital or to meet or work with anyone other than one that you had known for centuries before. But for me things were to be different from most others in my locality. I was born into a fairy-tale lifestyle of local fame and fortune. My dad was larger than life, outwardly happy, chatty, and charming. He looked to be living life to the full.

He was a millionaire a few times over by the time he was thirty, having first started out in the manufacturing of stainless steel products before moving on to other similar businesses and finally building large commercial and private buildings all over Europe. Shortly after I was born he sold his stainless steel business for a sum of money never seen or heard of before.

He drove a beautiful top-of-the-range Mercedes with a black leather interior that always made me sick on long journeys. The smell of leather mixed in with smoke gave my tummy the twirl each and every time. Once retching was inevitable, Dad would pull his car over to let me out to vomit only to light up another cigarette while casually observing me, and again another one on my re-entering the car. It was the early seventies, and children were to be seen not heard and certainly not to be thought of. If I got sick that was my problem, and if he wanted to enjoy the finer things in life—well, that's exactly what he was meant to do regardless of how my tummy reacted to such luxuries.

My dad took good care of himself. He worked and exercised hard and provided well for his wife and his family. The only other thing my dad liked to do was talk and drink in between a dinner of mostly T-bone steak. My dad was a particularly lucky man, as his wife was beautiful, one of the most beautiful of them all, and best of all he was completely loved by her.

My mother was the best singer in town. I can see him now leaning his head back over his sumptuous couch, his eyes closed with just his right hand gently out front swaying back and forth in time with the music. He was following tradition, Irish tradition, but he was doing so in style. Where others failed at gaining access to plenty of money, this was not so for him; he had that conquered.

My dad preferred the old Irish tradition of sitting around the fire, where you told or sang stories of the Great Famine, of lost love, or of young folk leaving for foreign shores. While there was television, older folk still had a preference for each other's company. They had their dreams; they had their hopes; and in Dad's time it was just possible to attain them. So he got to remain in Ireland.

Dad was surrounded by spacious living rooms filled with silks and velvets. He was the lucky one, the one who got away from all past hunger and strife. He was deliriously happy, and it was with that happiness that he shared his drink and food with all who ever came to visit. All were provided for with a generosity of spirit for which the Irish are world renowned.

My dad was the toast of the town and maybe even the toast of the country, for he had also appeared on the cover of the *Time* magazine. It was to be the epitome of his career—that one piece of paper confirming to all what he knew. He indeed did have it all—beauty, intelligence, and a gentlemanly spirit. He provided employment to hundreds in the locality and beyond in many counties where jobs were hard to come by.

He was keeping the married men of the region in jobs close to their own families. Irish entrepreneurship was an unknown entity in Irish history at the time. It was this that gave him more glory than he was capable of dealing with, particularly one who knew little of the drawbacks to being ascended to such heights of adoration.

He was listened to because of this "placing"—the pedestal that society had bestowed upon him. His words were carefully scrutinized for any wisdom by everyone, except possibly himself. He was surrounded by warmth and hospitality from all in the hope that his luck would rub off and leave in its mist a trail of goodies. He was up on high upon a pedestal, and he simply loved every minute of it. It gave him the confidence he might not have otherwise had. It gave him a sense of false everlasting harmony. Slowly he stopped seeing what was ahead of him. He lost his keen observation skills, the very ones that had made him the man he was.

My mum met my dad at a dance at the tender age of nineteen, and by the time she was twenty, they were expecting their first child. The Catholic Church viewed this as a sin—to be pregnant outside of wedlock—and so, just like everyone else in this condition at the time, they were quickly married as quietly as possible. It was this or a life sentence in a Magdalene Laundry for my mum, where the newborn could have been taken from her and given to an infertile married couple.

The Catholic Church also told her not to use contraception (for it was a grave sin—I still felt this "condemnation" at the age of seventeen), and so we continued to arrive one after the other quick in succession; and all had limbs and arms where limbs and arms were supposed to be.

Upon marrying she was forced (by the law of the land, right up to 1973) to give up work in the local bank, as it was her duty to rechannel her young life of freedom and fun into a life of rearing children and being wife to an upcoming enterprising husband. After her seventh child, she was exhausted; but more important, she was fat.

She tried every diet in the book: the grapefruit diet, the grape-only diet, the F-plan diet, and the last-resort no-eating-and-plain-starvation diet—everything to remain within the clasp of beauty. And all of this for her successful and by now popular young man, one who left earlier and earlier each day and who would return later and later each night—all for work-related pleasure or pain. What did she have to worry? Couldn't she always leave him if she was unhappy?

Of course she could not, as it was unheard of. There was no divorce back then; only the carefree and frivolous had thoughts such as these. To stay was a matter of pride and principle. The bigger the sacrifice you made for God and your country (and your man) the more you would be rewarded in heaven and for eternity. These were the teachings of the Catholic Church my mother grew up with.

But somewhere along the way it was becoming obvious to those who cared to notice that my dad was, as the Irish saying goes "losing the run of himself," followed quickly by "Sure isn't the money such a curse?" Some would reply, "Ah well, better not to have it." And that's what the church told us too: that to fly in the face of God—by being too rich or too happy as this was to be seen as too selfish—would have its consequence.

But my mother continued to do what she always did—she stuck staunchly to her routine. She continued to diet (badly and unsuccessfully but results were never seen as a lesson onto itself), bought even more fabulous clothes, dyed her hair an even stronger shade of blond, and finally, when all of that wasn't enough, she joined him. She joined him because she could not beat him into staying put. She followed him everywhere just like my earliest memory.

He told her he loved her; wasn't that enough? He told her, but soon after he stopped coming home in time for dinner, and when he eventually did arrive home he was drunk, so drunk that all he did was repeat over and over again how much he loved her. Eventually that's all we heard too. It got him off the hook, those little drunken words of love.

And in the latter years when she wasn't able to be out and about with him, she enlisted us to follow and bring him home—each and every one of us all at different points in our lives. Drink consumed our lives so much so that by the time I was seven I remember clearly waking up in the morning to a bottle of Hennessy closely nipped in behind the big black boiling kettle of water. I knew the portion of brandy to pour into the tea once brewed and to leave it on either side of the bedside table before heading off to school.

By then I had my very own personal school driver who just so happened to also be my teacher, she who was always lovely to me and she who relished each piece of Waterford crystal Mum gave her every Christmas for just such a consideration. She too was in awe of my mum and dad just like everyone else in the town. The internal troubles we as a family were experiencing were not yet public knowledge.

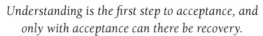

> *Understanding is the first step to acceptance, and*
> *only with acceptance can there be recovery.*
>
> JK Rowling,
> *Harry Potter & the Goblets of Fire*

Chapter 2

Abuse of a Different Kind

*O*ne day back in the summer of 1974 my dad was outside tending to his lawn. I had been born early in the year, and my birth had timed perfectly with the move into our big new house in the countryside surrounded by two acres or so of greenery and fencing. The house was so big that it looked out of place, so the only thing to do was to surround it in shrubbery and give the place a feeling of maturity.

The story goes that Dad was attempting to do some planting of trees near the front fencing when a man pulled up in his small little orange Fiat and started to holler at him—initially from afar, but it wasn't long before he was right before my dad. He told him in no uncertain terms that he was making an absolute mess, the complete opposite of his intentions. "A gobshit," I think was the word used. The man pointed out the things Dad was doing wrong at that time. That man was, shortly after, to become one of Dad's top maintenance foremen (covering work and home improvements) and subsequent friend, and that's just how things were done back then.

My dad loved him instantly. He took the same approach as my dad, with his bark being much bigger than his bite. Like my dad he oozed get up and go; he spoke up for himself and had the appearance of looking like he knew what he was doing. He took the shovel off my dad, showed him the right way to use it, and then threw it down on the ground. Job done. I can still hear my dad laugh and joke as he told me of how he first met Dan Reynolds.

Dan too had a large family and was hard working and gutsy. Unlike Dad he didn't have oodles of money, but in his favor this fact didn't stop him from doing what he believed was the right thing to do—correction—where he saw the need to do what he thought was the right thing to do.

Dad had gotten so used to everyone bowing to his every need, including maybe even his lovely wife, that it was with great honor that he took good criticism from Dan. He knew he was out of his depth when it came to all things garden related, and with this in mind, he was only too delighted for someone to come along and point out what needed to be done and more important take over and personally see to it that the place was made just as it should be, reflective of our new status in society. We had finally made it, and our home was to reflect this.

In the years to follow, Dad ended up giving Dan more than just the sought-after position of foreman; he extended to him and his wife and family our very famous family welcome. He brought him and his family into our family fold. He brought him in to the inside. We were told in no uncertain terms to treat Dan and his family as one of our own, and in return Dan too treated us as among his own. The one thing that never crossed Dad's mind I'm sure was the need or thought to protect what he had. This was to be the story of his and my life thus far.

*   *   *

He was always in my head, then and now. He was like a father to me then. "You were just a day old when we first had you," he used to say to me, loving the way that made me feel. He knew I adored him. He knew I loved him. He was better than my dad, you see. He was around. He was available to me. He loved being with me. He loved to see me go for his pocket and pick out my favorite sweet, the famous green-covered Emeralds. He would then pretend surprise when I went back for more. He was everything to me. He was everything my dad wasn't.

He brought me everywhere with him; I loved him for it. There was always something to look forward to when Dan was around. Some weekends it would be for a trip to see the latest flowers and shrubs in a gardening center, sometimes clothes shopping just for me as a treat. Other times we would spend Saturdays on a little boat in the middle of lakes fishing, others on the bog turning turf. But the days I loved most of all were when we would walk the nearby canal following the cruisers through the canal locks giving the odd helping hand. There we would walk hand in hand or sometimes snuggled up close on his bicycle, but always we were together, Dan and I; we were one.

So when he took me into the garage one day like any other day, I was on top of the world. I felt special. For once in my life, I was getting the attention I had so long craved. I was like putty in his hands—I was just five. He knew this of course, and so he made sure to make best use of that very thing in every possible way.

He turned gently to me this day and said, "You know French kissing is big everywhere at the moment; it's the latest thing. Would you like to know what it is?"

I jumped with glee. I couldn't wait to find out. I pleaded innocently, "Please Dan, please Dan, show me. What is it?"

His reply was quick and terrifying. He bowed down over my five-year-old body and swept me up in one swift movement with his arms around me as if for one of his big bear hugs; the ones I knew he loved to do in front of all his family and in front of my family too; the one that showed how much he loved me and only me.

But this time he went a few steps further. He passionately stuck his tongue down into the depths of my mouth for what seemed an eternity. I remember that I couldn't breathe. I was suffocating, and I couldn't get my tongue out to tell him. I remember how his tongue felt as if it were today. It felt old and withered. It felt wet and dirty. I felt dirty.

When he finally stopped, I was numb. I was in shock. I didn't know what to do. But he did. He turned and asked, "Well now, did you enjoy that? Wasn't that something?" I nodded, glazed eyes fixed to the floor. I needed air. I started to move toward to the garage door to where the fresh air was, where I could breathe again. I began to sway my way there. Dan gently took my hand as if to help and walked me back outside. He was acting as if the world was his oyster, like he was as happy as could be. He began to whistle. Art, Dan's youngest son, was just finishing unloading blocks from a trailer outside; when he saw me, he quickly looked down, continuing on with his work.

From then on Dan hung around my bedroom window every morning he could—there was always some handyman work to be done to our new home—tapping gently until I would finally relent and let him in. He would snuggle in passionately, kissing and feeling me all over—happy with his fix. I would turn my head away as soon as I could, letting him do what he needed to do. I craved his attention, but somewhere deep inside I knew not in this way. I felt uncomfortable with this level of closeness, but as of yet I did not understand it.

Within a year, Dan had orchestrated a situation where I would spend every weekend and summer with his wife Nell and their family of five, three boys and two girls. One member of the family was nicer than the other. Eimhir, the youngest girl, was the one I most adored. My own home always seemed quiet in comparison and lacking in any real warm. All of my siblings were in boarding school, giving my parents all the time they needed to drink.

Dan's home quickly became my real home. It was where I was happiest. In Dan's home I was center stage. I was the one who got to lie up beside him in his big foldout chair perfectly positioned before the television. I felt comfortable in his arms in front of his family in front of a warm fire with lovely yummy food in my belly. Nell was a great cook; she made me scrambled eggs in a cup and lovely fluffy potatoes with gorgeous homemade soup on top. All her food was wholesome, just what I desired.

One night after my usual routine of falling asleep and being put to bed, I awoke suddenly to Eimhir's cries of protest. Dan's arms were wrapped around me, and he was taking me out of Eimhir's single bed, one we happily shared together. Eimhir was like a big sister to me, a loving one too. She took care of me and happily brought me everywhere with her and her first boyfriend at the time. They both were so kind and attentive to me.

I can hear Eimhir's words ring in my ears now as I look back. I can see what she was trying to do for me. "Ah Dad, leave her be here with me; she is fine here. Look at her. She is sound asleep. Leave her be." He said little by way of reply. He had his hands on me, and nobody was going to keep me from him. I was around seven at the time. I was big enough to know there was something peculiar about what was happening to me. I could sense Eimhir's worry.

Dan brought me to his own bedroom where his wife was asleep in one bed, a small double one. This was right next his son Art's single bed. He put me on the outside facing Art. He cuddled into me, and quickly I fell back asleep. I woke up a while later to feeling something wet in my pants. I didn't know what it was. Somewhere in the back of my mind, I had this vague sensation at my lower back, which now I know to be a penis in a relaxed state.

The next morning when all had left the bed, I put my hand down to feel inside my pants. Everything had dried, and my legs just felt a little sticky. I got up, cleaned myself, and went out to play with Art and his best friend for the day. Dan had already left for work.

I remember playing at the back door while Nell was beside me washing all her boys' clothes; they were man-sized jeans and tops, and they were always dirty from the type of work they did. The older boys, one nicer than the next, were all either working manual labor or driving trucks. This day Nell was very angry with me I could tell. I wasn't quite sure if it had to do with the work she was doing or if it was something I did, but for some reason I got a sense it was to do with the latter. She threw me dirty looks and for a time hissed at me like a snake. I couldn't make out what she was saying, so I just turned and ran out the door. She never did this again.

Many years later I talked to my counselor about this strange reaction of Nell to me. On describing the events as above she told me that it is very common for the wives of those addicted to have this reaction. It is what makes up part of their denial, and in their denial they have the ability to see things as they need to see them as opposed to seeing them the way things really are.

It was important for her at the time to see me as the guilty party and not her husband, as that was her own way of survival. I found this interesting, as it correlated to more than just Nell; it correlated to every woman I knew, of which there were many, who found themselves in the same situation. They (and me too) did everything to make the situation as they wanted it to be, including lying to themselves rather than facing the truth.

My relationship with Dan continued for some time in the same vein where I would be awoken, taken away, or quickly grabbed at any time of the day or night as Dan's needs dictated. To be honest, I have blocked many of these memories out, and I am very happy that I have. There is nothing for me to gain from remembering any more detail than I have already; the damage has been done.

One day, without any notice, my mother blankly refused to let me go to Dan's house one weekend. Many years later I was to find out it was because my Aunt Bridget—who lived close by—had just found out about Dan's abuse of her child, and so she had insisted that my mother keep me away from him. I on the other hand had become so attached to Dan and his family that I was distraught to find out that I was not allowed join him, and so I ran away into the surrounding fields heading in what I thought was the direction of his house. I earnestly set about clambering over wired fencing and streams to catch him.

My eldest brother, Tom, who happened to be home that weekend from boarding school, followed after me. Being twice my age he caught me with ease and dragged me all the way back effortlessly with one arm; he was striding his way quickly home when my Aunt Bridget greeted me with her arms held tightly behind her back. She had sent Tom out after me. She was more of a disciplinarian than my mother; in fact she was quite the opposite of my mum, which needless to say, since I was not used to it, caused me to be terrified and in constant fear of her.

Tom dropped me promptly in front of her. There was rage in her eyes. This anger didn't take long for her to show as she swiftly took her left arm from around her back and brought it crashing against my little face. It was loud and sharp. She didn't have to say anything. The slap had said it all. I fell into my bedroom close to the back door and waited patiently for my mother to come to me. When she finally did, I said sorry. She nodded her acceptance with gentle eyes and left.

Dan's abuse of me stopped thereafter. My mother never discussed these details with me. Dan continued on in our employment, and my parents' relationship with him was as it had always been—friendly and loving.

* * *

A few weeks before my Holy Communion, I arrived home from school to find that no one was home. My teacher, Mrs Dolan, had dropped me home as usual. As I waved good-bye to her I jumped enthusiastically over our cattle grill before running down around our sweeping driveway to our back door. I tried opening the door, but it was locked. I peered through the kitchen windows; all seemed quiet.

I searched for a key to the door everywhere I could think of: through the boiler house and out beyond the walls of the house. I could not find one. All the usual haunts turned up empty. I then tried all the windows; sometimes one was left open wide enough for me to squeeze through, but this time they too were all closed.

I gave up and turned, taking the path outlined in the grass leading to my neighbor's house. I wandered down enjoying the sun and wind and each little flower as I went. I could tell it was spring.

The summer was just dawning. I turned a bend and moved swiftly through the open back door. It was dark inside, so I waited for my eyes to readjust. It was then that I saw Jonathon, the neighbor's son. He had also been my brother Tom's best friend before Tom left for boarding school. They were both eldest sons. Back then, this meant they were automatic heirs to the throne. They were in control.

I told him my parents were not home. He didn't seem too worried, so I joined him in the settee room to play for a while. He started to tickle me. He had done this a few time before, and each time I felt uncomfortable. It was always a little too intimate. Suddenly, he just picked me up like a little rag doll. I thought it was to throw me up and down and tickle me some more, but instead he carried me to his big cushy armchair. He tucked me in like he was settling in for the night. Instantly I shivered.

His fingers moved randomly inside my pants. I pulled away. I tried to look at him. I wanted him to see that I was afraid, but he didn't take my look. By now, he seemed to be a trance. My body started to shake. He loosened up briefly only to pull me firmly back inside the hook of his arm. His hold on me was so tight that I found it hard to breathe. His fingers played around my clitoris. A dirty smell began to permeate the room all around us. He continued until he penetrated; I fainted.

I arrived home later—I don't remember how—and for a long time I just stood at our back bathroom mirror. My parents were still out. I remained standing in front of the mirror for some time, looking directly into my own eyes, intensely so.

I remember repeating over and over again, "I can't deal with this now. I will deal with this when I get older."

A few weeks later I celebrated my Holy Communion. I do not remember any part of this normally humongous event for any child, particularly for us girls who get to dress up in a beautiful white dress for the day. I have photos taken on this special day; I just have no memory. I know I will never get them back.

Just after my communion my schoolteacher upon passing my desk, stopped and sniffed all around me. She slowly lifted off the top of my desk, putting it onto its hinges to see what was causing the smell underneath. There neatly stacked up one on top of the other were a few weeks supply of mushy green sandwiches staring right back up at us. She was shocked. I was too, for I hadn't even remembered putting them there.

If you had asked me at the time if I was okay, I'm pretty sure I would have said I was perfectly fine. I was studious, diligent, and considerate, maybe just a tad more quiet and a tad more thoughtful than most. But that was it; otherwise I was pretty normal.

I didn't have a repeat incident with Jonathon again. I simply refused any further visits to his house, a decision that did not raise any questions on my parents' part. I never thought to confide in them about what happened; it would be some time yet before I knew what exactly had happened.

I did, however, come to dread Saturday mornings, as Dan would periodically arrive to do his chores. My mum as always made tea and sandwiches for him, instructing me to bring the tray out. One day I refused, but she insisted, telling me that I had no manners. Again I refused, saying that I didn't feel like it. She then clipped me on the ear. I walked away. A few minutes later she arrived at my room and asked me again. I took the tray, laid it outside on the short of the grass, hollered at Dan, and then disappeared back inside. She never asked me again.

I knew at the time that my mum was afraid to go outside our back door. The only time she ever left the house was with Dad; otherwise she remained inside. Angela, the head of our family, had by now taken over a lot of the responsibilities that would otherwise have been Mum's. Angela was by now in her early twenties and working as a secretary in Galway City, having left boarding school nearby a few years earlier. But each weekend she traveled home in time for the weekly shopping trip into town. She also used this time to pay off any bills that needed attention. Even though we had a second family car, my mum wouldn't drive it; but Angela did. Eventually it was to become Angela's car as my mum ceased all contact with the world other than with Dad.

Over time it became obvious to all my siblings and me that Mum needed drink to relax her before she would depart her home for anything, and I mean anything. The fear of doing so was too much, and so drink was used to alleviate this terrible illness that had taken a firm grip of her. Like my dad, she couldn't cope without drink—the need for it just manifested itself in a different way in her.

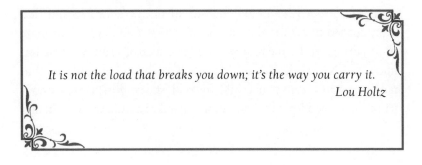

It is not the load that breaks you down; it's the way you carry it.
Lou Holtz

CHAPTER 3

My Mum

I was eight when I first saw the characters Tom Sawyer and Huckleberry Finn on television. Before long I was imitating them. Whatever they did, I did. I followed their every move. They were my heroes. I looked up to their carefree and independent spirits. They were determined to have fun. They knew what they wanted and were clear about where they were going. No task was too tough and no mountain too high.

Early each Saturday morning while Mum and Dad were still asleep, I would tiptoe down to our kitchen and steal a few goodies from within the hidden chest of our big orange drawers, the sneakier the better, the quieter the better. I didn't ask; I stole. And that in itself was an adventure. I would then take out my little red scarf from underneath my clothes and discreetly wrap all my goodies in it.

Every now and then I would glimpse behind to see if anyone was looking. Luckily, there was no one behind me; I was safe. I would then carefully tie my little red scarf onto one end of a long bamboo stick I had stolen from outside. I had taken it from one of those fancy trees in our well-tended gardens. This was a tough job, but only the tough survived.

When this task was complete, it was then time to head off out onto the rolling plains of endless countryside, just it and me and nothing in between. It was time for my next exacting task. I would endeavor to climb endless mountains (hills) and cross and crisscross over dangerous tracks of swollen river, crashing over giant stones and stumbling over small pebbles—all but to stop awhile for a bite to eat on the other side.

This is the life, I thought to myself. Could it get any better than this? Here I was at one in nature and in all its beautiful surroundings. I didn't have to think about anything else. I had no need. It was simply my adventure, and I was safe here. This was home to me. The beautiful rolling countryside and I were at one.

*   *   *

As Dan's influence over my life went into decline, I began to join my mum on the odd shopping trip—this was before my mother's self-imposed imprisonment in the house—to exclusive boutiques and department stores many miles away. We would come back laden with all sorts of the finery that was to be expected of a millionaire's wife and child. I was dressed in all sorts of funny-looking clothes fit only for royalty. Some kids in my class were lucky to have shoes; one didn't. He came barefoot to school.

I had more than one pair of shoes and more than one fancy dress too. I wore them to school, as there was no such thing as a school uniform. I got nicknamed "Tin Man" because of my dad's company. Everyone knew our name; everyone knew we were a success. I just wanted to fit in. I craved a best friend; as of yet I didn't have one. So when playtime came round I would get down and gritty; I played football with zest just so I could get dirty.

One day I observed my male classmates playing football in the sun while the girls were inside sewing. We were finishing off our new outfits. Mine was purple and white. It was two separates, a long skirt and a sleeveless top. They were just completed, and so we each got to wear them to show each other. Then it was break time, so we left them on and went outside to show the boys.

There was one boy in particular who fancied me; he always tormented me for a kiss. He was rough with me and didn't understand the word no. I didn't particularly like him because of this. But also he told me that Santa wasn't real. I was devastated, so I decided not to believe him. I was still young at the time, too young not to believe. Even I knew that.

Out of nowhere he swooped upon me. I jumped with surprise. He tried cornering me for a kiss. I held my hands and arms up high as if to hide behind them. I was protecting myself. He stood barefaced in front of me with his legs wide apart. He was determined. He leaned in and whispered to me, "You look nice in your new dress." To him it looked like a dress. It put me into a bit of a huff.

I reacted angrily. "It's a skirt and top," I hissed before I darted past him and ran for my life. He followed, chasing after me. He knew that he was faster than me. I knew it too.

I decided to do something I had never done before. I jumped the perimeter wall and ducked down below it and into the field behind the school. I kept running for my life, my head trailing just below the wall line. I was trying to vanish out of sight. Before I knew it there was a gang of boys following me. They weaved their way quickly toward me from all angles across the field of corn. I was tired; I needed to catch my breath, so I bent down and hid.

Suddenly a boy jumped me. He pushed me to the ground facedown. Others followed suit. It was hard to breathe. They ripped away at my new clothing, taking shreds here and there. I heard them jumping and screaming wildly with excitement. It was fun to them. Thankfully a teacher came to my rescue. I heard her shout at the boys, "Get back inside the wall *now!*" She kept shouting while everyone looked on. One by one they disappeared back over the wall and back into the school grounds. I got my chance to move. I sat up and looked down at my new clothing; it had been ruined. Tears welled up inside. I ducked back inside where no one could see me cry.

I went home that evening feeling low. The boys were mean to me. I hated them for it. Discipline in schools back then had been a beating with a stick; it had made the boys themselves particularly rough and heartless—like tigers trapped in a cage. They had ruined my pride and joy—my very own precious piece of clothing. My teacher tried to fix it up, so I put it back on; I remained determined to fit in. My teacher dropped me at the top of our lane that evening.

I slowly walked down with my feet trailing behind me. I longingly looked up through the trees. I gazed admiringly at the strands of sun shining through the branches. It all looked so beautiful and serene. I made my way to our back door, my heart traipsing behind me (it's a real Irish saying "traipsing"). Just as I got to the corner I heard a noise. Someone was shuffling about in the laundry room; it was an outhouse connected to our back door via a small glass walkway. It was Mum. I could hear her moving back and forth close to the doorway next to me. I quietly walked around and stood by the doorway. It took a few seconds for my eyes to readjust to the dimness. There was just one small bare bulb dangling from the ceiling throwing off little light, with cobwebs all round.

She was sorting through an insurmountable pile of laundry. She was fussing about in an angry sort of way. She was bent down like an ostrich in the sand with her body facing away from me. I peered around her to see what the fuss was all about. It was cold and cramped inside. There were stacks of clothes everywhere; some were peering out of giant-sized black bags, and others were piled high in different-colored baskets of all shapes and sizes. Loose clothing too was sticking out from every angle. They had simply been thrown anywhere they could fit and just left there.

At times the washing machine and dryer stood idle. Then one-day work would recommence. This was one such day. She was in the throes; usually it started by separating out the retrievable from the irretrievable. Those that had slowly turned into a permanent mossy shade of green were quickly stuffed into black bags and stacked on top of the giant freezer that had once been of use. Next was separation by color—where she was now.

She looked up and saw my shadow. It was a disappointed look. It was always a disappointed look when she saw me and not Dad. I knew that this particular task annoyed her. She loved other tasks, but not this one. She loved hovering and dusting. She loved when all was clean, when the floors and the furniture were free of stains and the countertops were shiny and bright. She loved when all was sparkling like new (this too became her addiction and ours too—as to be clean was to be perfect, perfect enough to warrant love and attention).

She would have the television or radio on while doing these tasks. She sang in tune with "One day at a time, Sweet Jesus, that's all I'm asking from you. Just give me the strength to do every day what I have to do. Yesterday's gone, sweet Jesus, and tomorrow may never be mine. Lord help me today; show me the way, one day at a time." I loved to hear her sing this song. This meant all was happy in her world. I could tell that it took her mind off things. It kept her busy. It distracted her long enough till Dad could make it home. When he came home, there was no need to distract. There was no need to sing or clean. He was back.

I looked dirty and sad. I patiently waited to see if she noticed. She didn't. I waited another minute and gave up. I blurted out, "They ripped my new outfit, Mum. Look at it. They ruined it. Look. They all chased after me and knocked me down. They really scared me." She turned briefly as if to inspect it. It was a casual look. *Maybe it is the fact that they are my clothes and not hers,* I thought to myself. Maybe these ones were not as important.

She made a move to exit the room before stopping to query, "Who did it?"

I cried, "The boys in my class, Mum. Wasn't that mean of them?"

She looked again. She hesitated, smiling at my innocence before dismissively saying, "Serves you right." It was an angry statement; she was always so angry with me—either angry or drunk. She continued on inside to the kitchen.

I knew to leave it, so I too turned and wandered off. I remained alone in my thoughts on the back lawn nestling down by the riverside, the grass underneath my pillow. I gazed longingly back up through the moving clouds. I wished to be up there covered in their cloak. Later Mum called me for tea, but I didn't budge.

*   *   *

Summers were spent in County Kerry in our summer home. Again our home was plush and opulent and always without food. I never knew where my parents were from one day to the next. My bedtime story entailed my taking a last-minute dash to the local hotel to catch Mum serenading Dad. As I weaved my way toward my Mum to say good-night she would gently open her eyes and smile before closing them again, continuing uninterrupted in her song of love lost. It was then home and into bed till morning came where the day started all over again with a fresh delivery of tea and brandy to either side of Mum and Dad's bedside lockers before I headed off on one of my very own adventures.

Usually it was to hang out with a group of girls and boys from the neighborhood. We would walk the roads for miles around, take a swim, and then head back home in time for tea—compliments of a piping hot bag of chips from the local takeaway. After, I would watch from outside as my friends would all disappear one by one inside while I continued to wander around outside, sometimes hanging by their bedroom windows till late in the night. This daily routine never changed. There was no other plan.

One day, I remember that Mum and Dad drove past me out the entrance of our estate. I had a look of bewilderment on my face as they slowly drove by without stopping. I waved wildly from behind for them to stop. Mum's electric window slowly came down, and out popped twenty pounds. The electric window slowly went up again, and off they went, two lovers on their merry way.

Many years later my sister Joan told me of a story of how when she was young she too ended up in our summer home for a month on her own with no money (at the time I thought it was just me). On rejoining her, Mum was only interested in flaunting

Jean Berry

the thousand-pound coat she had picked up along the way in a very famous local boutique called Danielle's. It was one of the more famous shops in the country at the time, known for its hefty price tag and corresponding exclusivity.

My mum was not worried about Joan's welfare any at stage—not when she left her, not when she returned to her, and not even in between. Joan told me that at one point around this time the mothers in the local neighborhood had a quiet word with our mum to tell her that it was a disgrace that her children were allowed out all night at such a young age. Mum seemingly, according to Joan, reprimanded us and put us on curfew for one night and then gave up. Boundaries were not to be a feature of our childhood in any shape or form.

* * *

One day, when I was ten, Mum and Dad took off and didn't return for a long time. It was during the school year and not long after my granny (Mum's mum) died. She had been living with us for a year. It had been one of the happiest times of my life. I would run home and rush up to Granny's room to get her dressed; then I would comb her long, shiny gray hair up into a bun in time for a late lunch. Usually lunch consisted of a hard-boiled egg with a little bread cut into small pieces. She reminded me of a helpless little bird, a very pretty one.

After just a few hours in her electric chair, she would feel tired and head back to bed. I would follow shortly thereafter, and we would each take turns saying the rosary till in no time at all we were both fast asleep—I in a permanent foldout bed at the bottom of hers. One night I heard her cry for my help. She had fallen just inside the door of our bathroom, the en suite. She didn't want to use the personal alarm Mum had rigged up beside her bed. Instead she asked me to quietly go up to my mother to let her know she needed help getting back into bed. That was that; there was no more to be done—there was no moaning, there was just quiet.

It wasn't long after this that she passed away peacefully. There was no fuss as she patiently waited till every last one of her children made it to her side—one got delayed on a plumbing job—before falling off to sleep. I was deeply saddened by her passing, but I didn't show it or act it. I had never thought to go to my granny for help back then or anyone else for that matter, as it simply wasn't the done thing. Elders were to be respected and listened to, but never did you dare reveal your secrets to them. I only remember seeing my mother's pain at this time—amid the drink. It was like that of a yearning as described in those old Irish ballads—for a time lost.

And so my mum and dad just up and left for Asia, I think. On this particular occasion while they were away the second-eldest sister, Maria, was supposed to be looking after me, but I wasn't even too sure as no one mentioned anything. It's only now as I look back that it is obvious that she was meant to. Anyway, it wasn't important, because she didn't have to. By this time I was well capable of looking after myself. On the outside all was right with me, so my sister left me to myself a lot; she had just fallen in love, and like my mother, her eyes were only for her man.

At this time I lived off fried potatoes and custard, and I cooked them myself. After dinner as a treat I would sing for hours on end, singing the entire Madonna album over and over again, her first one. I would position myself directly in front of our big, black oven doors, my hairbrush tight against my lips, its handle in my right hand posed as a mike. It was then that I would notice the reflective glass of the oven glazing lovingly back at me; I had company at last.

I remember making an effort to shower once a week. I think I did so to go unnoticed; it was my way of fitting in. Each morning I cheerily went to school. It never occurred to me not to go. I was good academically, so maybe this was the reason why. I was consistently top of my class. I excelled in mathematics. I simply loved everything about it. My teachers at this time were particularly good, and so I soaked up their structure and clear simple approach to life—work hard and all will be good in your world.

At night, I was terribly lonely. When darkness came, I was unbelievably afraid. It would close all around me like a blind. It caused me to feel claustrophobic. I would brush my teeth, scrub my face, and slip silently into bed quickly mouthing my prayers and hoping they would let me sleep. Most of the time sleep wouldn't come, and so I would peek outside waiting and praying for my sister to come home early. She never did, and so my little body would then slink back down from underneath the curtain lining.

I would wallow a little to myself before turning and heading, downcast, back to my bed. Then amid the safety of my covers, I would curl up tight and act like I didn't exist; all lights were switched off so that no one could tell that I was home alone. This was my newfound protection at this time: the undercover of complete darkness—my breath was careful and slow and everything still and quiet.

At the time I was living in the back bedroom of our house. It was the room next to the kitchen and back bathroom, next to the back door and outside laundry and boiler house. Lots of doors! At the far side of the house was our greenroom encased in glass. It was around this time that I started to have nightmares. One in particular still haunts me even to this day.

I am in bed, my body rigid, its outline imprinted onto my mattress. Suddenly my eyes shoot open wide. I stare steadily into nothing but blackened darkness. Before my eyes I visualize a man quietly but meticulously breaking in through the glass door at the far end of our house. The glass shatters before me now, its splinters flowing like a river everywhere around. His first few steps crash resoundingly over broken debris their sound faint but deadly clear. I know him, yet his face is hidden from my view. He is big, much bigger than me, and he is cold and dead inside. I feel a shiver run down my spine.

Slowly he knowingly glides his way through open and closed doors, his every move vibrating powerfully off the carpeted floor and slowly stealing into the very corners of my mind. My heart flutters wildly; it is not sure if it can make it to the end. It is ready to surrender. It is ready to give up. Gleefully he takes his time. He is in no hurry; there is no pretense—he is here just for me. His breath is heavy, his body tight with rage. He makes his way along our bedroom-lined corridor, narrow and endlessly long. Then he swiftly maneuvers through our brown swinging doors, holding them steady as he passed. He knows their every move, their every creak. The sounds of his steps become steadily heavier and louder as he begins to near close.

He moves past our main hallway before his final descent through the kitchen door and out through the back kitchen door and into my bedroom. He stops just inside my door and glares through the darkness into my very soul. I do not stop him. I am frozen with fear; his every breath bangs against my throat. I wake up screaming as he straps me to my bed and gently but deliberately in one stroke cleanly slits my throat. Blood gushes everywhere. It is painless in the end, my body limp by his side. He gets his way; he always does. I am helpless. I am alone.

I didn't tell my sister I was having nightmares. By then I was living inside myself. I had stopped talking; I had stopped trying to communicate. Instead, I got lost in my dreams and my adventures. They were always there for me—not like my parents, as they were never anywhere to be seen.

*   *   *

In the same year when my granny passed away, I got my wish for a best friend at school. Rachel was her name, and she along with her family brought me everywhere. They would drop me off at our big front doors and would rarely be invited in, nor would they want to come in. I always went to Rachel's house. She never stayed overnight in mine, even though my house was much bigger and grander than hers. My house was every kid's dream, but her parents were wise; they knew all was not what it seemed.

Both her parents had alcoholics in their family of old, and so they often would say, as would Rachel, that "drink is a curse." They thought it best to take the pledge at confirmation, committing before God never to touch the drink. Rachel had me convinced at this time that this was the only way to go, but I chickened out at the last minute; she didn't. She was trying to help me as best as she could. What she was asking of me sounded scary and unknown at the time.

I guess as of yet I didn't view drink like that. I didn't see drink as my parents' downfall. I just thought they didn't love me; I thought I was an unwanted mistake that came along five years too late.

In fact for many years, for reasons unknown to even myself, I thought I had been adopted or left behind by a relative. My mother often talked of a cousin of hers who came to live with her and her family growing up—as that is what they did back then, particularly if coming from a large family or if one of the parents had passed away while the kids were young. For some reason I picked this up as if this was what happened to me too. I guess it was a feeling I had because I always felt different. Maybe it was to do with the fact that by the time I was six, I had been left behind as all my family disappeared, going to boarding school. In reality I had connected much more with Dan's family than my own from an early age. To me, he had been my real family.

When it was time for the sister closest to me, Joan, to go to boarding school, she simply left, and as sisters we went from sleeping side by side to simply not seeing each other for years. She went her separate way and I went mine. We didn't meet up again till I was in my late teens. As she was leaving boarding school, I was entering it. She has often mentioned since that she does not remember me growing up, and I too felt this way. We were like swinging doors; we all just came and went without a thought or care for each other or for each other's feelings. I couldn't tell you one thing that my sister Joan was good or bad at, what she cried at or was happy with. In fact, I don't even remember what she looked like back then.

And so when it was time for me to leave primary school to go to secondary boarding school I just up and left Rachel behind without a care in the world. Leaving her behind had little impact on me, but for her, as I found out through her mum many years later, it had been devastating, with many nights of sleepwalking followed by many nights of tears. It didn't cross my mind to remain in contact. She wrote to me; I just never replied. As a family we never did that.

*   *   *

Just before departing for boarding school, the same one that all my sisters had previously gone to, there was a flurry of family weddings. First my eldest sister Angela married her long-term boyfriend Julian. It was like a royal affair. As this was to be the first family wedding, there was endless discussion about the guest list. The wedding was big, expensive, and lengthy. It ended after three whole days and nights of celebration. I just remember seeing lots of bodies all over the living room floor and guitars thrown here and there.

At this point Mum and Dad still had the appearance of money. Dad had by now completely lost the ability to focus on making money and was now simply living off his millions. But through its constant misuse it was showing signs of rapidly dwindling. Angela did all she could to manage my parents' money for them, but on marrying she finally relented control and happily returned it to my uncontrollable parents. It had been a terrible stress to her growing up; she was tired of carrying it along with my parents.

Next was Tom, the eldest son of the family and God to Mum and Dad. Tom learned early that he was up on a pedestal, just like my Dad, and nothing to his mind was going to bring him down. Just as he was getting used to all the freedom this kind of guaranteed future can bring, Tom's new girlfriend Jane became pregnant. As she was slim (and breathtakingly beautiful, of course), she hid her pregnancy for a long time. She was too terrified to tell her dad. When her pregnancy became evident, there was an uproar in her home. It was then that they were discreetly married. My parents were relieved to see an end to this conflict. A beautiful brown-eyed baby boy was born a week later.

It was then the middle child Liz who married. I didn't know till years later that she too had become pregnant outside of wedlock and so she, like Tom, was discreetly married while just pregnant. This was all only a few months after her best friend from boarding school, Jane, did the same—by now Tom's wife. Angela oversaw both marriages. Both were also rushed off to commence married life elsewhere. For Tom that was Galway City—Dad had set up a business for him there. As Tom wasn't the one actually pregnant—it was his wife who was left with that scar—he didn't have to quite leave the country. Liz did and so moved to Scotland the day after her wedding.

Of all my sisters I had felt closest to my sister Liz. She was naturally motherly—giving hugs and kisses freely to me and my other siblings. Years later, she told me that it was intentional and in stark contrast to how her mother treated her growing up. She vowed early on that she would tell and show all around her how much she loved them so that there would be no confusion. I cried profusely on the day of her wedding. I could not bear the thoughts of us being separated. It was on this day that I had just found out she along with her then husband Shane, Tom's best friend, were moving away for what I thought was forever.

Our second eldest Maria at this time also found out she was pregnant, and rather than face the same end, she chose, after a brief chat with Angela, to terminate it. Thereafter, she left for Canada after her then boyfriend. A year later, she married and a child followed suit.

Of all the marriages it was Tom's that showed the obvious early sign of failing. Like Dad, he was always teetering on the edge, living life "out of control," and unlike Mum, Jane couldn't handle it. In his world, he had nothing else to do but wait for his inheritance. As a result, his business quickly folded, as he didn't have the ability or the interest in managing it properly. After a number of drunken and violent outbursts on Tom's part, he and Jane separated. Up to this point in our family, we had been exposed to drunken people everywhere we went, but we had never been exposed to violence in the way Tom showed it. This was a line that had never been crossed before and one we weren't going to cross either. As a result, Tom became isolated from our family unit. His aggressive behavior was viewed without question as unacceptable.

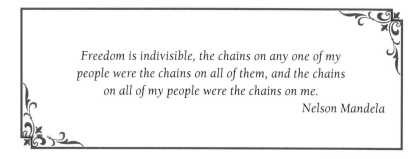

*Freedom is indivisible, the chains on any one of my
people were the chains on all of them, and the chains
on all of my people were the chains on me.*

Nelson Mandela

CHAPTER 4

Opening Up

Summer 1989

I found my way into my sister's room for comfort, unbeknownst to her. I sat on the end of the bed, in the center, and looked miserably toward the closed curtains to my left. It was dark and gloomy out, just like my mood.

I heard a shuffle and a big bang before me, so I turned back around toward the bedroom door to see Liz come bursting through. She startled me, as I was not expecting her. I jumped a little. She was otherwise occupied. She gave a quick glance at me, probably wondering what I was doing in her room.

She looked again, slower this time. I knew that she noticed something out of place. I said nothing. I looked down, trying to pretend everything was okay. She came close to me, sat down beside me, and observed silently for a time before turning and gently asking, "Are you okay?" I remained quiet. I was not sure how to reply. I didn't know how I felt. I was afraid I would never feel again. I had become numb. I was cold, without a heart.

I sharply replied, "I will be fine," my head slightly downcast. I was serious. She did not stop; she probed a little more intensely. She did so in a kind manner. Maybe she saw something in me that she saw in herself. "You know you can tell me, Jean. Whatever it is, you can tell me," she said shyly.

I remained still for another long while thinking, *Do I trust her? Can she really help? Am I better off killing myself? Maybe that would be easier.* I didn't know how to say what I was thinking, because no one had ever asked me before. All I had ever known was a drunken dad, a depressed mum by day and a drunken mum by night, and lots of drunken relatives.

I didn't know how to express myself, but I had to say something. I had to tell someone. I had to talk sometime. Surely this is as good a time as any? She seemed nice and warm. Maybe I should give her a chance to help me; maybe she will? I blurted out, "I have been abused," and continued to look down. Thank God I finally got the words out. Thank God I knew what had happened to me. What a relief. I didn't even know where those words came from; but somewhere deep down I knew something terrible was wrong with me.

She looked at me in torment for some time before she asked, "Who did this to you?"

I replied unequivocally, "Dan."

"What did he do to you?" she queried meekly. I wasn't sure how to answer; I didn't know exactly what he did. I didn't even know that as of yet I had blanked most of it out. I just knew what bits I remembered weren't right. "He touched me," I said embarrassingly. Maybe I did something wrong that made him think it okay to touch me in that way?

But she obviously didn't think so, because she hugged me tightly for what seemed an eternity. It was the first real hug I had gotten since we had last met. I had been to visit her with Mum and Dad when her firstborn, Beth, arrived. But this was her first visit home since she had been forced to depart a few years earlier. She was still angry, I could tell. She talked often of how Angela had made her wear a wedding dress she hated and how it had all been dealt with so heartlessly. She didn't like Angela as a result.

It felt so good to have her hugging me that I turned and told her what else I had been holding onto inside. I looked up at her and said, "Jonathon touched me too." She looked away, startled, and then hugged me some more.

She let go of me then and said she would talk to Angela (there was no one else in our family to talk to). "We will sort this out, Jean. I will get back to you," she said. We talked little after that. I didn't remember leaving the room or what I did next. I just remember that I was relieved that I had finally got those hideous words out of my mouth and thanked God that for once I didn't feel dirty inside.

* * *

A few days later Liz and Angela called me in for a chat. Instantly I felt an icy shiver run down my spine.

Angela was in a hurry, I could tell. She usually was. She had lots of things on her mind too; there was always some trauma around her that needed fixing.

She rushed to my side but came to a halt before me to turn and look back toward Liz to check that she was in tow. She was almost nun-like in posture, her head facing down, her eyes avoiding mine. I was in the same position as before, sitting at the end of the bed—my eyes were dead, my soul tormented.

Angela turned her head back around toward the door to ensure that it was closed. Both were in position side by side: Angela in front, Liz behind. They had serious looks on their young faces. I felt tension fill the air.

Nervously Angela said, "Well, the good news is that I have talked to Dad and he has had a chat with our neighbors, and, well, the good news there is that Dan has been let go so he most likely won't get to anyone else. Well, that is if he hasn't already got to them."

It was instant. I felt my tummy inside beginning to do its twirl. Everything was becoming hazy; I was flitting in and out of consciousness. I stared blankly back at her and began to go into a trance. How come I didn't feel any better? This news was like a knife through my heart. There was no justice in her words, no kindness, and no compassion.

She didn't see any change in me. She quickly brought the conversation to an end and switched back to her own lighthearted busy schedule. "Well, that's that then. Okay, I'd better get going. Julian is waiting for me at the front door, probably hooting his horn as per usual, and you know what he is like, always late for something."

From somewhere deep inside me I found my focus. I didn't know how or why, but I looked up one last time and questioned softly, "But what about Jonathon?"

She turned to Liz with a little look of surprise but then replied almost instinctively, "Oh, don't worry about him; he was just experimenting." And that was that.

Our conversation came to an abrupt end, just like the way it had started.

There was no hug, no question, and no hope of any follow-through or positive result other than for other potential victims close by. It was completely authoritative in its approach with not even an ounce of feeling—just the way everything in my family was dealt with back then.

They both quickly turned away, whispered something about counseling, and departed the room we were in, the same room where I had first opened up my heart in just a few days before. I remained there in a haze, wondering where it all went wrong. It was all too much for me. I decided not to look for any more answers.

From the edge of the bedroom door, I saw Angela go into Mum and Dad's room, which was next to Liz's. She talked briefly to someone in the shadow of the door. I saw Angela from behind. Afterward, she turned, smiled, and breezily waltzed out the door. I heard the front door slam shut as if she was in a hurry.

I stood glued to the ground. I had nowhere to go. I had nothing more to say. My parent(s) disappeared further into the shadow of their room, out of sight completely. Everything went blank.

*   *   *

After that day, my sister Angela and her husband took me under their wing and tried to help as much as they could. My sister Liz returned to Scotland, although I don't remember her departing. In fact I don't remember seeing Liz for a long time after.

One night when Angela returned from a night out, I went into her kitchen, hysterical. When I calmed down, she gave me a brandy. I then told her how I had tried to take her husband's sleeping tablets in the hope that I would die. She laughed, explaining to me that they were herbal tablets and that I would have needed six times the number of any other tablet to have the effect of just one. She then put me to bed and told me that sleep would do me good. We have never talked about that night since.

In the early years Angela would periodically bring us as a family on long walks up the nearby mountains. Sometimes we would bring a picnic with us, and the whole family, minus Mum and Dad of course, would sit and chat aimlessly for hours on end. Those were happy days. My last memory of Angela being the kindhearted person whom we had all grown up with in those early years was on my eleventh birthday when she surprised me with an old ring belonging to her. She had it altered to suit my finger. It was one of the most thoughtful gifts I have ever received in my life.

But that was the old Angela, thoughtful and kind. Somewhere along the line that broke down in all the chaos that endlessly followed us all around. She grew tiresome from carrying us all, and she had every right to be—she had been given nothing but responsibility from a young age. She had no childhood of her own. She has never looked back since. She was simply too tired to.

Instead she turned to having affairs, one after the other. You could tell that it made her feel young and carefree. She talked incessantly to me about them in a humorous "hush hush" way like young girls do when they are telling each other their very own special secrets. Many a girlie mid-morning coffee focused on her long stories of infidelity and nothing else. She liked being the center of attention; she craved it. It took over her whole world and, for a while, my world too.

This turned me into a closet full of secrets. I was beginning to feel overloaded with everyone else's secrets, including my own. The piece that confused me then was how when I compared hers with mine, I saw her issues or secrets more or less in the same light. I could not differentiate what she was doing to her body from what had been bestowed upon me. Sex to her became a joyful ever-increasing addiction. It became her only focus aside from the mundane routine and responsibility of married life.

At this time Angela suggested that we start up a prostitution business, just two of us to begin with. It was said jokingly, so of course she thought this was a great way to make money and all at a time when Mum and Dad were extremely tight for cash. It was also at a time when she obviously thought she might as well get paid for having sex seeing as that was all she could think about. I remember her face; it was unapologetic and completely analytical in its thinking. She was more than capable of doing it, and she had no qualms about who she brought with her either. She had no qualms about anything like this.

Before I returned to boarding school, Angela organized a counseling session far away in Galway City. It happened to time perfectly with a girl's night out that Angela had planned directly after my meeting. At the meeting the counselor asked me a little of what I wanted to discuss. I didn't know. I wasn't too sure what had happened to me other than somewhere deep down I felt it was wrong. At this point, no one in my family had told me that anything was wrong. I then asked the counselor if it was okay for me to be upset. She replied by saying that everything was "relevant"—for example, she had just had a lady with her who had been terrible upset at the sudden loss of her cat.

I tried desperately to grasp what she was saying; at the time this comparison didn't make sense. How was what I had been through the same as a woman grieving over a dead cat? By the end of the session, she seemed almost agitated with me—most likely because as of yet I couldn't remember much of my childhood. At this time, I had blanked a lot of it out. After, while partying with my sister Angela, I concluded that counseling was not for me. Angela was happy not to have to pursue this. She had enough on her plate—getting to and from Galway was a just another chore to her.

After this, I became anorexic. I plummeted to ninety pounds in the space of three months. I lived off a bar of chocolate and little else a day. I was afraid to drink juice for its calorie content (and I knew the calories in everything because of all my mother and Angela's diet books). I survived off water mainly and the odd can of Diet Coke. Weight and controlling it became my addiction. Everything around me was overwhelmingly confusing. No one was communicating with me. I saw little reason for hope.

This all took place just as Jonathon was getting married. As we were close neighbors, all of us were due to attend. It was a much-talked-about event, as was any celebration that revolved around drink. On the day, I wore a navy and white polka-dot top and matching trousers that were in a size eight but wrapped around me like they were a size twenty.

Of course, my Mum and Dad never noticed that I was anorexic. The rest of my family did but never made the connection with my newly revealed childhood trauma. Instead they all focused solely on my weight loss. They couldn't see then what I saw. I saw that I had been perfect as a child in beauty, form, and in my studies; it had been easy and natural for me. But in my teenage years this all changed, as my body changed. I began to struggle to maintain this level of perfection. In a desperate attempt to regain control of my youth and of my image of having once been perfect and so lovable, I stopped eating. Going back to being "perfect" gave me hope that someday someone would again love me in a way that I craved.

I realize now that even though Dan's love was wrong, it was the only tangible love I had known as a child. My subsequent realization of how he had abused his position to manipulate and abuse me left a void deep inside me desperate to be filled. I stopped eating because I craved love and attention, and like my mother had taught me, I was at the time willing to do anything for it. Like her I kept falling into the trap of creating drama in my life to distract me from the real issues upsetting me.

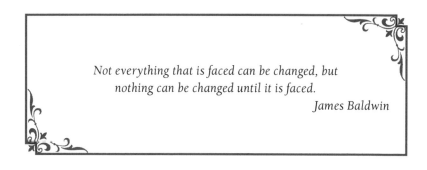

Not everything that is faced can be changed, but nothing can be changed until it is faced.

James Baldwin

CHAPTER 5

Boarding-School Days and a Second Opening Up

I used to pretend that I loved boarding school, when in reality I hated it. Pretending to be brave was always important to me. My sister Joan, the second youngest member of the family, didn't feel the same way; she was honest about boarding school. She hated it from the very moment she entered it at just eleven. Our sister Maria dropped her off that day, and from then to the end she hated it. She was bedwetting at the time and continued thereafter for some time to do so. She was also teetering on the edge of obesity. Unlike me, she ate her way through her emotional problems.

What Joan and I did have in common was that we both knew that there was no point in saying anything to Mum and Dad about our feelings, as we were never listened to. There was always some important money dilemma overshadowing every part of our childhood, so much so that I knew we were always in "financial difficulty." In the end I dreaded boarding school because I knew that

Mum and Dad couldn't afford it (they had money at this time, but mainly it was in property and so we were always waiting for the big windfall that would follow a long drought). We were always a year or two behind payment.

Early on I made some friends, but as time went on I quickly became more and more reclusive and so often found myself sick with depression. The rigid structure of boarding school was hard to adjust to given my extreme freedom before that point. The principal at the time, a nun who had a soft spot for me, arranged once for me to go home for a few days after one such bout of sickness/depression. Instantly I picked up in form and well-being. On the way to the bus station she turned to me and said, "Well, now I know what was wrong with you; you are just homesick!" If only she had known—I didn't know anywhere else to go.

I remember having a friend whose father asked her to write to him each time in a different language. Each letter she wrote came back corrected with the words she had gotten wrong highlighted in red. It was their way of staying in contact. I had no contact, none whatsoever, ever. My parents dropped me off on my first day in our fancy Mercedes with Mum dripping in jewels and a full-length fur coat, and from that day to the next I did not receive one phone call from them—about anything, not even when my dad's mum passed away or about the selling of our home. Nothing was ever serious enough.

The building itself was cold and imposing, with long winding high walls and black iron gates. Inside the stone exterior was nothing but wood; even the walls were of varnished wood instead of wallpaper. There was a high-ceilinged music room placed appropriately at the very front of this monastery-style building with a grand piano and an orchestral organ fit for a king. While there was a little dust here and there (there never was at home.) everything appeared clean and orderly with a wooden cubicle and basin ready and waiting for each one of us freshmen among the many corridors and stairwells doted here and there. There was little obvious structure or layout to the building, with extensions seeming added on in bits and pieces over many years, each highlighting a new direction—one was for a sports arena, another a study center, and yet another a rectory.

The hardest thing to adjust to from early on was the resounding high-pitched school bell. It chimed throughout the monstrous building almost every ten minutes in the morning, telling us when it was time to get up, then get washed, then get dressed, then get to Mass, then to breakfast—and this was all before school, which took place two stair flights below our living quarters. The bell even rang at the exact time when we were to go asleep.

On my weekends off, I took a bus home followed by a taxi. Most weekends I arrived home to closed curtains. Mum was inside, deeply depressed. She would ask me to find Dad. I'd walk back into town and work hard to cajole him to come back home with me. I didn't succeed most of the time, so I would leave him with his friends in whatever pub he had frequented this time round. It was always the same few. He would arrive back late, falling out of a taxi. I would walk out when I heard the taxi pull into our yard and help carry him to bed.

Mum made one appearance in all my five years at boarding school, and that was only because I begged her to. I coaxed her into coming to a parent-teacher meeting; it was one leading up to my intermediate certificate examinations. I was excelling in school at this point. This was my first official state examination in secondary school, and so it was a particularly big deal for me—there was only the final examination, the leaving certificate, after that.

But Mum couldn't control herself and arrived in drunk with my aunt by her side; she had come in support of her own daughter, my first cousin Annie whom I rarely saw or talked to; she was leaving just as I was entering. My aunt was perfectly sober, but my Mum was not. I ended up being mortified. I had to look on and endure in front of all my friends and teachers as my mother swayed from one side of the room to the other with her mouth reeking of alcohol, with little or no sense coming out. I never again asked her to make an appearance on my behalf.

When examination time came round, a nun came up to my desk to check to see if I was cheating. On entering boarding school, as was normal in Ireland, I had completed an entrance exam in English, Irish, and mathematics. This is to determine your suitability to either ordinary or higher-level study from this point on. I had come from a school that had been ahead of its time academically, having completed English (yes, direct from England) state papers at the end of each year. This was not normal at the time, but my head teacher had been particularly forward thinking and pushed us all to the limit in our studies and sporting activities. As a result, I felt that I had completed these strongly.

Subsequently and surprisingly I was assigned to ordinary level in all subjects. I knew this was not a reflection of my true capabilities. Of course back then you did not disagree with your superiors, so instead I worked hard and managed my way up to honors level in all subjects before my first year came to an end. My math teacher in particular saw my potential—she insisted that I be moved up after just one day.

So when this nun, Sister Carmel, confronted me in the middle of my geography intermediate examinations, I said nothing. I just stood up and looked on as she shook every piece of paper she could find on my desk and clothing. It was embarrassing, but I didn't let it get to me. I still got top marks in all her classes—in fact she was the only teacher from whom I ever received A's. I probably looked like I never paid attention in her class, as I mostly never did, but there were two reasons for this. First was my eyesight. I couldn't read the board, and it never dawned on me to just sit in front of her—that wasn't a cool thing to do. The second was to do with my auditory-processing disorder. I was always shy from a young age about the pronunciation of words either in English or any other language (learning my native country's language, Irish, was a disaster for me from day one), and now I know that it is because I don't hear sounds the same way as many others.

I have to work at hearing "the sound or phonics" in every word. It takes a lot of effort, so much so that early on I gave up and instead quickly learned to utilize my photographic memory. I could repeat pages word by word. I can still to this day remember my little red spelling book and exactly where the word "Sword" is on the page. It wasn't till many years later that I also found out that my sisters had never done as well academically as me—lucky for me I had been sent to a different primary school from them, and my primary school teachers were much better than my sisters' were.

After a strong intermediate certificate, I decided to change direction. I didn't know why at the time, but it was the summer of 1989 when two things happened to me. The first was that I had opened up to my sisters about my abuse to no avail, and the other was that I fell in love. I had experienced my first kiss in Kerry that summer, and it had been heaven. But what I thought was eternal love was just a fling for the young man, and in the end I was left with a broken heart, heading back into school.

In my younger days I had got lost in books and television series of the Famous Five, the Secret Seven, and Huckleberry Finn. I also remember my mum giving me one very poetic and symbolic story to read, which I did over and over again—*The Diary of Anne Frank*. I instantly felt an attachment to her. Her story had a profound effect on me. I couldn't believe that we could all simply continue on as is in a world where people did this to each other; it was totally alien to every instinct I had inside me.

But this time round I decided to read Mills and Boon tales of romance. I dreamed of falling in love and being carried away forever more—my "knight in shining armor" protecting me from life itself. When he didn't arrive, I became disillusioned and started to act up a little in school. I got suspended for a week. I didn't seek permission to go to the shop at the end of the laneway. I didn't have to worry about the consequences at home; anything I did meant very little. In fact I got to spend a week at home doing whatever I wanted. I came back wondering why I had not done it sooner. It was around this time that I began skiving from my classes, a very hard thing to do you would think in boarding school, but I found lots of ways. I conned my way out of class and back to my bedroom, where I continued to read endlessly. It was all I did except play tennis.

In fifth year I was picked for the senior tennis team. I was ecstatic! In an effort as part of the "first" team—I was anorexic at the time so this was a big effort—I rang home to ask for money for new runners and gear. Everybody else on the team had them, and of course I wanted to be like my teammates. My mother told me that she simply didn't have the money for them. I said nothing. A month later I rang back, undeterred, and told her that I need money for new books and that the nuns had asked me to ring her about it; she sent the money. I was beginning to understand what I needed to do to get what I wanted. I understood that whoever shouted the loudest won; whoever didn't, lost.

Being anorexic was a difficult condition for me. There were lots of days of feeling like I was permanently going to faint. Eating was always an ordeal for me, especially as we had set times and were assigned to tables alongside other classmates. Eating was a very public affair. At home, it had been easy to skip meals, as no one was focused on my welfare. But being in full view of authority and classmates is an anorexic's worse nightmare. This meant pretending to eat while not really eating anything. I shuffled everything around the plate a number of times and took really small bites of everything. In the end, everyone was scrutinizing my every bite, and mostly I was unaware, as I was almost too weak to eat in the first place.

As time went on and I became progressively worse, the girls from all the classes had become knowledgeable about who I was and what I was doing to myself. I became a focal point of many conversations. Afterward, my classmates told me that I was a very scary sight on the tennis court as the racket and ball loomed over me; everyone could see the racket was practically heavier than me. You could see clearly through my legs; not a pretty sight!

During this time, my sister Angela and brother Joe came to visit me as often as they could with bags of sweets in tow. They both worked close by. Dad had also by now financially supported Angela in setting her up a business in Galway. Later on, Joe, in between Liz and Joan, joined her. Joe had dropped out of boarding school early. He simply kept running away. Eventually my parents gave up trying to keep him there and instead put him to work. Years later, we were to find out he had taken this action to avoid being sexually abused by a brother/priest.

Slowly, over time, I worked my way out of this disease, not through any obvious process or trained intervention. It was just I got tired of feeling faint all the time (and hungry!). I clearly wasn't getting any extra attention from Mum and Dad, so it had all been in vain really. Its effects—continuously dieting by way of attaining perfectionism and so worthiness of love and attention—didn't leave me for many years to come.

In my last year of school, undeterred and with no moral guidelines, I went on to more daring tasks as a way of earnestly trying to get attention. One such task was organizing nights where we would sneak out of boarding school—every girl's dream, I'm sure. Along with my friend I would ring early in the evening for a taxi to collect us from the local pub less than a five-minute walk away. When darkness fell and all were asleep, we would simply walk out the front gates in all our finery and wait for our taxi. This in turn would bring us to an all-night spot in the west of Ireland. We moved from one club to the next, dancing and laughing before heading back by taxi to the back of our school. There we would have our uniform ready and waiting in plastic bags hidden in the bushes.

Quickly we would change, jump over the perimeter, and proceed to pretend jog along the path outlined, all the way back to our shower rooms. Once washed and dried, we would join in with others from our class in time for Mass. We would then spend the day laughing and joking before finally snoring our way through choir practice; thankfully this was always the last class of the day.

Naturally when my mock leaving certificate results appeared they were not what had been expected of me. I remember that my by-now old mathematics teacher came up to talk to me. I was managing to do honors still, though I was continually absent from class. She said in a loving and concerned voice, "You know, Jean, you really should be doing better, results wise. I know I don't teach you anymore, but I know you are better than this. I know you are an A or B student." She hit a cord with me, and I started to cry. She was confused at first, but then something twigged within her. She touched me, said nothing, and left. Shortly after, I completed my final state examinations and left boarding school with a bag and no plan other than to move in with a friend nearby. I quickly secured a job locally too in a Pizza Hut.

A week or so after the leaving certificate results were issued, my mother appeared in Galway one day to meet up with me. It tied in with a business meeting Dad had to make. She asked to view my leaving certificate results in print (there was no e-mail back then). It was quite out of the blue, and for lots of obvious reasons I wasn't really expecting her to. She had never shown an interest in anything I did up to this point. I was delighted though that she did ask, as I still craved her love and acceptance.

I remember where we were standing when she turned to me and nodded. We were just inside the back entrance to Brown Thomas on Shop Street; it was a cold and windy wintery day, and the heavy door slammed shut behind us. I didn't quite pick up what the nod meant. She asked to view my results. Like Angela, she was as always in a hurry. We were meeting Dad shortly in a pub around the corner, so she waved her hand impatiently as if to signal me to hurry up. I did, and I took them my results out of my bag and handed them to her without delay.

She examined them closely, thought for a moment, and pointed, "That one there and there, we'll make them As instead of Cs. We'll tell everyone you got two As and the rest Bs and Cs." And that was that. We moved through the swinging door into the shoes and handbags department, leaving the cold behind. Mum got herself one or two small items of clothing that day. I didn't get anything. We met Dad in a pub close by for a drink, and then I left. There was no conversation around my future or my plans, and there was no advice. The only focus had been on what to tell the neighbors about my obviously much-asked-about results.

Shortly after this, Eimhir, Dan's daughter, rang me to say her dad was dying and that before he went he would like to meet with me. I arrived home for the weekend and went directly to Dan's home to see him. He looked happy to see me. He didn't have a guilty look, so it was obvious from the onset that he was not going to say sorry. I wasn't sure why I went except that being with Dan's family always brought me great comfort—as they did on this day. All were thrilled to see me, asking many questions as to my whereabouts and what exactly was happening in my life. It was so refreshing compared to going home.

I had very mixed feelings as I left Dan's bedside that day. I knew that he was very close to passing away. I also knew that he had no concept of what he had done to me; it was obvious that no one had confronted him in any way that might make him see the light. One thing that stood out was Dan's wife, Nell. Just like my mum always stood by my dad, so too was Nell sitting right by Dan's bedside, ever faithful to a man who was never faithful to her.

The part that pained me the most was seeing Eimhir once again. It had been a few years since we had caught up with each other, and each time she was even more unrecognizable from her pretty and outgoing younger years. I had stayed with her and her husband a few times two years earlier, and in those brief meetings, I had a sense that he was abusive to her. The extent of it I did not know, but seeing her at this time, it was obvious that she was a broken lady. She did little to engage with me and appeared totally disillusioned. I was relieved to find out that she has since separated. It angered me to see her this way—for she had been one of the most loving and beautiful women in my life thus far. Even then I still didn't think to open up to her about my sexual abuse. I guess maybe I knew it was a step too far; it was too close to the bone.

Dan passed away three days later. I attended the funeral with his family. I was right by their side the whole time. His sons seemed in good spirits and by all accounts were moving on with their lives. Dan's eldest daughter, who had left at fifteen, rarely returned but did on this occasion. Her husband and their two beautiful children closely guarded her every move. I could tell that she was curious about me when she met me. She was looking for some signs of something untoward. I didn't give anything away—but neither did I cry at Dan's passing. Like the boys, I was lighthearted and happy.

The following morning, I was back home lying in my bed with my windows and blinds open listening to the birds outside. It was sunny outside, and for some reason I was feeling good in myself. Dan's departure had brought some kind of closure for me. It was like I knew that he could never touch me again for sure. This happy feeling was rare for me, so much so that I decided that this was as good a time as any to have a heart-to-heart with my mum. I think possibly the closeness I had felt with Dan's family made me crave the same with my mother. I also thought that I was coming to an age where we could talk maturely about my childhood trauma. We were now to my mind meeting on the same level at last.

I politely asked my mother to join me in the kitchen, having heard her bedroom door open close to mine. I told her that I had something important that I wanted to say to her. She was coming down to make the by-now usual cup of tea and brandy for her and Dad. I kindly asked her to sit down beside me at the kitchen table. It was a long one, but I made sure we were close, as I didn't want to have to shout.

I started to talk, saying, "I love you, Mum." She didn't reply.

I paused before continuing. "I have something important to say. It's about my childhood, and I was sexually abused. I was sexually abused by two people." By now I was shaking like a leaf, as I began to wonder if I was doing the right thing. But somewhere deep inside, I was very proud of myself for having the courage to utter those famous words locked in my head, all less than two years from my brief and cold encounter with my sisters.

My mum looked at me blankly and said nothing.

She continued to look at me blankly for a few seconds more before she stood up and walked in slow motion to the kitchen countertop, where she switched on our big, black boiling kettle. It was always boiling—ready to make the tea. She turned, I thought to come back toward me, but instead she walked right past me. She kept walking; there was no turning around and no stopping. She quickly exited the room and didn't return. I was left alone once again.

There were no hugs, no tears, and no connections. There was just a wide chasm of silence, one that I had been born into and continued to live in. It was everywhere, this silence, and it was not a kind one. It was like I was not worthy of attachment or feeling; I was less than worthless.

*   *   *

At the end of the summer, after thinking through my options—I didn't have too many—I took up studying business studies in a private college in Galway. I knew deep down that it was my last chance to get out from under Mum and Dad's feet, but my heart was never in it. Instead I used the opportunity to experiment and socialize, anything to avoid the pain of my mother's denial of my truth. I began to follow in my sister's Angela's footsteps, one of the best socialites I had ever known up to that point.

Like her, I too took it upon myself to socialize in the vain hope that I could blot out my past. I did everything I could to distract myself. I played with drink, drugs, and men. I kept going till I could think no more. If I could have gotten hooked on drugs I would have, but for some reason they just didn't suit me. My system would go on shutdown every time I tried hash or grass. I would be sick for days on end, and anything harder scared the hell out of me.

For a time I shared an apartment in Galway with a girl from boarding school. She had been the year ahead of me. We had always got on well. She was more mature than me, so I let her lead the way in exploring our sexuality and youth. We went from party to party and back again. We even threw a few. Eventually it came to an end. My sister Liz, who was home briefly for a visit, arrived up to tell me that Mum and Dad were worried about me. The college I never attended must have made contact with home, letting them know that I was not attending. It was only midway through my first academic year.

Liz, the by-now responsible one of the family, made me feel guilty for letting Mum and Dad down—there is always someone to let down if you want there to be, including ourselves—so I promised her I would give college another go. But I didn't mean it. I just said it to keep her happy. At this point an apartment Mum and Dad owned locally became free, and as a means of saving money (I was a terrible financial inconvenience at this point), I moved into it as Liz suggested. My friend moved with me, but instead of paying my Mum and Dad rent, she paid me the rent money directly.

At this time I also began living "off the dole" (government funding for unemployed) as a means to an end. My eldest brother Tom was in the same boat—he just wasn't even pretending to do anything else. Tom was also living in the apartment with us, but he was mostly away with his best friend and drinking buddy, Liz's husband, Shane, who was by now a regular traveler between Scotland and Ireland. Liz and her husband had returned to Ireland a year earlier. They had briefly lived with Tom and his then-wife Jane in Mum and Dad's apartment before moving to a place of their own nearby. It had given Tom and Shane a chance to rekindle their relationship. At this point, Shane, Tom, and my dad were experimenting with a number of startup businesses—Dad thought it best to get Tom and Shane working together—but nothing much materialized, and so Shane and Liz returned to Scotland a short time thereafter.

I remember feeling a tad bit sorry for Tom at this point. He could never seem to quite get it together—by now his marriage was well over. Maybe it was the fact that I felt the same way, deep down. At this stage, Tom revealed to me that he had sexually abused too, while in boarding school; so we had that very much in common.

One way in which we differed, though, was in our use of money. I had always been good with money with little or none of it. I made it go a long way. So much so that I used to loan Tom twenty pounds every single week out of my dole money so that he could continue drinking in the fashion he had become accustomed to. I see now that he must have been thrown money as a kid; I hadn't. I didn't see the signs at the time as I see them now. It was at this time that he was getting lost in addiction. I think I was just lost in depression.

Nothing changed for a time except that I quickly got caught and removed from the dole as being in college and "signing on" together was illegal—and so I went back to living off very little except what my friend was giving to me in rent. I continued from one day to the next in a blur and went from one boyfriend to the next; some were lovely and some not so. I didn't care. I didn't care if I lived or died. I was dead inside. My mind was dead and incapable of study, my heart heavy, but somehow, I don't know how, my body was still managing to function and go through the motions of everyday living.

* * *

In the intervening years, there was another incident, similar somewhat to the one with my mother at seventeen, where I made reference to my anorexia in passing with my mother. Only this time I heard my mother's voice adamant in its reply to me. She said in a very indignant voice, "You were never anorexic." I replied slowly and inquisitively, not sure where she was coming from, "Yes, I was, Mum. I was around fifteen at the time."

"You were never anorexic," she said again, like I hadn't heard her the first time.

Now I was really inquisitive. I decided to expand on my last sentence as if to justify to myself that it really did really happen, "Yes, I was, Mum. I went down to almost nothing. You could see through my legs. The whole school was worried about me. In fact I have lots of photographs to prove it—at Jonathon's wedding."

"You absolutely were not, never; that never happened," she replied sharply.

I decided to end the conversation there. I simply gave up. I was amazed and shocked at how much in denial my mother really was. I think somewhere along the line, I decided all on my own never to lie about anything. I had learned to hate her denial. I hated how she let it eat her up inside. I knew that wasn't for me. It was one of the few right decisions I made at this time. It is one I still live by.

After this conversation, I stopped trying to reach my mum. I knew it was too late. I knew she was too far gone; I had nothing to work with.

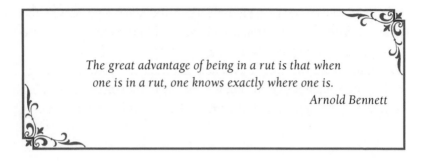

*The great advantage of being in a rut is that when
one is in a rut, one knows exactly where one is.*

Arnold Bennett

CHAPTER 6

The Summer of 1993

*T*he year 1992 had been a long one. I had finally relented to move home to Cork and start over. I was now back living with my mum and dad and getting ready to commence college in September close by. By now my parents had no cash, and so I was left relying on my sister Liz for handouts to make ends meet. Liz by now was the only one who had access to Mum and Dad's dwindling property portfolio, and it was on this basis that she was able to help me out. I was indebted to her.

Angela at the time had lots of money, having married well, but she was focused on trying to keep what she had close to her. I guess she had seen firsthand how badly Mum and Dad had managed their fortune and was making sure the same did not happen to her. She did, however, arrange local employment for me on a part-time basis; this was due to continue through my college years, and so began a good working ethos that was to stay with me.

The previous summer, Liz had returned to Mum and Dad's house without her husband. At the time, I didn't take much notice. She had just had her third child. I assumed that she was just home for the summer. But the summer at home led into autumn, the autumn into winter, and so on. Before I knew it she was still at home a year later. I didn't know the reason why, nor did I dare to ask. I also had enough going on in my own head.

It wasn't until a full year later, in casual conversation with Liz one night, that I got a sense of her circumstance. I can see now looking back that it was only by chance that she opened up to me and how desperate she was. She had no one else to talk to. Mum and Dad were no good to any of us. She had no one else to listen to her side of the story. She mentioned, while calmly lighting up a cigarette, that she had met up with Jane, our ex-sister-in-law, some days back. She was nonchalant about it, like it didn't really mean anything.

Jane, who was by now separated from my brother Tom, knew that Liz was living at home with Mum and Dad. Liz had told her so. Jane must have somehow concluded that things were not well between Liz and her husband. Liz was always slow to give anything away. She would prefer to hold it all up inside. She preferred to let it out slowly under the calm of the cigarette smoke as she exhaled. Even I smoked then (I was never really a smoker as they always made me sick). Living with Mum and Dad was a nightmare. There was no peace. I smoked back then for my sanity, as did Liz. She still does.

Liz's body was stiff as the words came out: "I always hated that stupid bitch for her lies." I looked a little surprised at her statement. She was angry, I could tell. It just wasn't like her to be this vindictive unless she was cornered. I knew that Liz hated to be cornered. She hated feeling like a caged animal. She didn't mind making tough decisions, as they were her tough decisions to make and not someone else's. This new information changed all the rules in her book. Now she was left with little choice.

I said nothing. I looked at her and waited. She blurted out the rest: "Jane said she wouldn't trust my husband as far as she could throw him." She continued, "Who is she to know? Well, who the bloody hell is she to know?" Jane told Liz some new information that she had not shared before. It was about Liz's husband—how she knew he had been unfaithful to her when they lived in Ireland previously; this was before the move back to Scotland a second time. In fact Jane suggested that Liz's husband wouldn't know how to stay faithful if he tried. She gave the impression that it wasn't in him, that he was too needy. She even suggested that he was messed up just like our brother Tom—that's why they were best friends. That he had an addictive personality just like Tom.

Liz was very angry with Jane for the offhand long list of accusations. She never liked this about Jane. They had lived together temporarily while both had young children and little or no money. It had been a tense time all round. Jane, on the other hand, thought she knew Liz enough to tell her the truth. She thought it was okay to say this given that they were now separated. "It's just the way she did it," Liz said, but then Liz always got stuck in the detail and not the message. To be honest I knew that neither the information nor the way it was said was good. Neither was good from anybody's stance. The truth hurt, but it hurt even more if you sensed that it was delivered with vindictiveness. I now know that it was Jane's bitterness coming out; she had a terrible time being married to our brother. But I also knew that what she was saying was the truth.

Suddenly something triggered in my head. An image came to the fore in my mind. The image came out of nowhere, like a lightning bolt. Liz saw this. She looked at me. She could see I was puzzled. "What is it?" she asked. I didn't know where to look. I wasn't sure I should say anything. Anytime I had said anything it was always irrelevant no matter how terrible the information was. I think I was afraid too. I see that now. She probed again. I stalled. She probed once more, "Well," she said. I looked guilty. I knew it. I decided it was best to come clean. I was not good at lying. In fact at this point in my life I wasn't too sure if I was good at anything. I felt like I was excess baggage that the world could do happily without. That's how my parents made me feel, and a lot of the time that is how my family still makes me feel.

"I have some information on your husband. I'm not sure you want to hear it," I said quietly. I didn't look up for a good minute. She nodded for me to continue. I did. I told her everything. I tried not to sound as bitchy as Jane did. I knew the bitchiness had hurt Liz. "I found Shane in bed with another woman. It was in this very house here," I said. "It was in the end room. The room you are now in." I continued to tell her generally how it happened, how I had arrived home out of the blue one day the year before, heard noises, and followed the sounds until I came to a room where Shane was inside with another woman. I let her know that Tom had also been present if she wanted to talk to him about it as well. I knew that he would have more detail than me, if she wanted it.

Liz said nothing. She just looked at me in disbelief. I knew what she was thinking. "Her Shane. Her Shane would never do this to her. No, not her Shane. The one that always made sure she had enough money to buy food for the kids. Not her generous, kind, loving Shane." She lit a cigarette. I did too. I wasn't sure if I had done the right thing at the time. Thankfully I don't think this way now. A silence followed. I knew that it wasn't good, so I said nothing further. Instead I quickly kissed her good-night and went to bed feeling sad and lonely.

I found out many years later that the reason Liz had returned home was that she and her three children had been evicted from their home in Scotland while Shane was in the pub drinking with his friends. She left Scotland later that day, having booked a one-way ticket home for her and her three young children, and moved back in with Mum and Dad.

*   *   *

Liz remained living at home for some time. She became pensive and introverted, but from the outside, it looked like she was getting on with life without Shane. Life had resumed some kind of normality for me as, for the first time ever, I returned home from college with curtains opened and dinner on the table.

This didn't last long, of course, as again without any notice my sister Maria, who had six years earlier moved to Canada, arrived home with child and also without her husband. She too commenced living with Mum, Dad, Liz, her three children, and me on weekends—all while not communicating why or for how long she planned to remain in Ireland. By this time we were living in a small four-bedroom house at the edge of Cork City. Mum and Dad had downsized as a means to access some cash—which was directly used to cover the mounting bills.

Personality-wise Liz and Maria were poles apart. On the downside, Liz was a know-it-all controlling type, while Maria was laid back and outgoing. Liz liked everything neat and tidy; Maria liked to be on the go, meeting people, and was always generally in too much of a hurry to clean up. Liz was a stay-at-home mum, the motherly type (Shane financially supported her from afar, just not enough for a house of her own) while Maria had to work full time to cover her own and her child's day-to-day living.

Maria also just happened to be a Miss World lookalike. Growing up, our eldest, Angela, did everything to put Maria down, especially in ways that prevented boys from falling for her completely. Angela was always very competitive when it came to men. She quickly dubbed Maria the "dizzy blond" of the family. I think this may had something to do with the fact that she looked great in a short skirt. In a houseful of women who didn't look quite so good in such skirts, she was belittled much and often. Always Maria appeared to laugh it off and continued on in spite of her mother's and sisters' protest to wear those lovely short skirts.

Everything Maria did began to grate on Liz's nerves. Liz thought fun was something you did once a year and continually reprimanded Maria like she was a child. Maria ignored her many belittling comments and would continue on as normal. Before long Liz convinced Mum to ask Maria to leave, which Maria duly did; she quietly moved to a rented home close by. Underneath, though, I knew that Maria was very upset; she talked often to me about it. I see now as I look back how unnecessarily cruel my sister Liz and my mother were to Maria. I also see how detrimental a lack of clear communication is to a family situation such as this.

Shortly after this Maria returned to Canada and went on to have another child. Maria's departure brought to an end a very turbulent and uncertain time in both women's lives. To me, it was one of my more enjoyable time periods of my youth, for I hadn't been left suffering with Mum and Dad on my own.

*   *   *

About a year later Liz got back with Shane. "He was a good provider," she said. I said nothing. It was no surprise; deep down I along with everyone else knew she had little choice, just like us all. A little while after that she approached me again in casual conversation. She told me that she never believed Jane. She was derogative in her approach. I got a sense that I was somehow implicated in this reference; it was like Jane and I were the same. She told me that Jane was the liar, and a bitch of a one too. She told me that she believed Shane.

She then told me that Shane was very angry with me. She continued, saying that she believed that nothing had happened that day. She accepted that Shane was in the room all right with another woman, but she believed that nothing truly happened. She felt that he had told her the truth, the real truth. It was almost as if we were all out to get her except Shane. Her approach was extremely hurtful to me, but I didn't argue with her; as per usual I stood and listened and accepted her version of the truth.

I felt faint and sick. All I knew was that she believed him and not me. She was completely dismissive of me in every way. It was I who was made to feel like a liar and not him. I was the guilty one, not him. This was my fault entirely. I was made to feel as if I had caused a rift between Liz and Shane, the indestructible Liz and Shane. I came away that day confused. I never mentioned this event again, and neither did she. She never thought to ask me any more questions.

From this day forth, the real Liz ceased to exist, just like Angela had ceased to exist, and a new even harder person evolved—one who had an attitude of "just get on with it." She was bitter for many years after this as she made reference to the fact that Shane apologized once and then told her it was time to move on. From that time forth if she would give advice it was along the lines of "put up or shut up."

After this Shane and Tom's relationship came to an abrupt end. Alongside this my parents' relationship with Liz and Shane grew even closer—financially to start with and later physically as Mum and Dad would end up leaving their home to move in with Liz and Shane.

Tom spent years after trying to tell us what he knew of Shane as if to warn us of his wayward ways from a business perspective as much as from a personal perspective. As a family we took it upon ourselves to completely ignore him. We believed Liz's version of this event and many other similar events over Tom's—even me, even though I had been present at this event. I never told my family of this conversation between Liz and me, and so I lived on believing all of what Liz said of Shane until this very moment—now I no longer do.

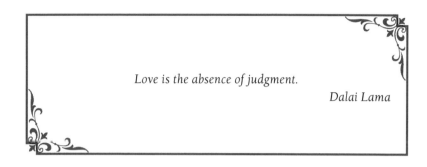

Love is the absence of judgment.

Dalai Lama

CHAPTER 7

First Love amid the Drink

I met Rob in a nightclub late in the summer of 1993. I was in Dublin for the night with my Cork friend Judy. I worked for her in the summer of 1990 in her office. We had gotten on well. I gained work experience; she gained a little social bird. At the time I loved to dress up and go out, and so did she. We had lots of fun times together. It was a summer to remember.

My weight at this point was back to normal after I had been anorexic for a time a few years earlier. Anorexia plays havoc with your metabolic rate, thereby making it difficult to stabilize your weight thereafter. I was—four years later—still struggling to maintain a normal weight given what I had done to my body. I was also still following in Mum's footsteps where there would be days of gorging followed by days of not eating. Overall though I looked healthy; as I look back I can see now that I even looked beautiful with a newly dyed head of blond hair. My hair had been naturally blond in childhood.

I remember looking over at a guy and thinking he was just gorgeous. I found out later that he was six foot four inches, much taller than me; I'm five foot five inches. He had black curly hair just below his ears. He had the college look, hip and trendy. He was slim with broad shoulders, just like every girl's dream. He was right out of my Mills and Boons love books. He was tall, dark, and handsome.

He looked relaxed as I gazed over. He was chatting away to his friend. He took a little look over at me; I looked back. For some reason—I don't know why—I decided to be cheeky, and I began to stare. I stared so that whenever he would gaze around I was looking right back at him, willing him on. He was smiling now to himself, an amused look on his face. I could tell that he was enjoying our exchange. I was too. It was lighthearted fun, something I knew little of until meeting Judy. She was like a breath of fresh air to me. I was light-headed on it.

Eventually though I grew impatient. I wasn't one to wait around. I began to look disinterested just to see if he noticed. He did, and so he slowly began to edge closer. Finally he turned around, but I didn't even give him time to speak. "You took your time, didn't you?" I said, looking directly into his eyes.

He looked back and laughed. "I sure did," he chuckled. It was a deep-throated chuckle. I had him hooked. "Where are you lovely ladies from?" he inquired.

"Not too far away, and you? What part of the world did you two appear from?" injected Judy, and thus began a very lively interchange between us all.

Rob as it turned out had gone to college in Dublin. He had just completed his accounting degree that very summer. He also had just secured a graduate position with a firm close to his hometown. All was set in his mind. He had everything he wanted. Now all he needed was someone like me. Well, that's what I thought, and do you know I was right. We kissed later that night on the way home. It was heaven. We then said our good-byes and arranged to meet the following day for coffee in a nearby public house.

The following day was sunny. I had gotten a spot during the night. I remember being devastated. How could I possibly look my best? I spend ages scrutinizing every part of that spot. Eventually I decided it was best to just cover it up. We were late for our meeting as a result. I had butterflies inside my tummy. It was the first time I had felt like this. Judy was right behind me. She was more excited than me on the outside. I was chuckling away to myself thinking that maybe it was she who had just met the love of her life. As soon as I walked inside, I saw Rob. He was sitting down, relaxed and refined, reading the Sunday papers, his cousin by his side. He had a lovely grace about him. Our eyes met. It was instant. I was in love.

Rob was in stark contrast to any man I had ever known before. He was consistent, loving, and extremely laid back in nature. There was no two sides to Rob; there was just him, no more, no less. He used to turn up at my house every Saturday afternoon just in time for the six p.m. news. There were no mobiles back then so he used to call me on our house phone on the Friday night before to confirm his arrival time of the following day. Even this call was consistent and considerate. In Rob, I found security and predictability, the very things I had been missing all my life. He had a calming influence on me. For a time, I forgot about my childhood trauma and focused on him instead.

We would head into town to meet up with my sister Joan and her boyfriend and do a mini tour of all the local hot spots. We always came back a little merry, and for a long time we slept in separate bedrooms. I loved the fact that he had no expectations or harbored any time pressure in sleeping with me. It was a relief to me and made me love him all the more. In the morning he would meet me for breakfast in the kitchen. He would then kiss me passionately good-bye before he headed his merry way back home. It was all so lovely and innocent. Just the way I wanted it to be. Just the way it always should have been.

At the time I was nineteen, and he was five years older than me. I was due to recommence college. Our rendezvous remained the same: in my parents' house, the same time the same day every week. It wasn't till many weeks later that we eventually slept together some time after college commenced. I made the move, not Rob. I remember it being shortly after he divulged this thought to me: "I think you are the woman I would like to marry." I thought him sweet and gentle, and so happily it moved us to another level of closeness.

The following Christmas Rob was made redundant from his job. This was replaced with good news shortly thereafter as an old neighbor of ours who instantly liked Rob on meeting him offered him a position with his consultancy firm. Rob was delighted to accept and so moved into my home with my parents. I was away in college during the week but returned one night during the week and again at the weekends.

A little while after this, at my request, my dad moved a double bed into my room. Neither Mum nor Dad made any issue of this. It was, however, at a time when Dad would often stumble in for a chat at any time when he felt like it come day or night. Normally it was to talk of days of old, of the people he had met and the fun they had, all the time laughingly telling how much drink they always drank. There were stories of weddings, horse-racing days, Gaelic football finals, lucrative business deals, and far-off trips to places unknown. He was like a child, one who forgot to ever grow up.

Rob used to laugh it off. He liked my mum and dad, as did most people Rob's age; to him they were very liberal. They were by then—accidentally I'm sure, as they hadn't been when it came to my sisters' and my brother's girlfriend's unexpected pregnancies. But times were a changing, and so were they—once their views and impressions of the world had very much been based on what others thought rather than any particular moral stance.

At the time my parents were entering a very dark side of their addiction. I would often come home from college in the early afternoon to find all the curtains pulled with the heat blasting through the house and Mum and Dad inside in their bed passed out with drink. It was becoming dangerous even spending the night in the house. One night Dad put a living room lamp on fire after having left his hat on top of it. The lamp had been on for ages beforehand, and so his hat stood little chance.

Another night their electric blanket went on fire while both slept quietly on it. I'm not too sure if it was Dad's cigarette or the electric blanket itself. Dad smoked one cigarette after the next always using the bud end of one to light the other while always forgetting to put any of them out. This caused a kitchen curtain to catch on fire once too. Dad in particular had become a fire hazard and required constant vigil.

Dad had by now become delusional from a state of constant drunkenness and went around mumbling and laughing mostly to himself. He had bottles of drink stashed everywhere, in the hot press, in the shower, behind walls—everywhere. We had moved to the house a good few years before this time. The bungalow itself was down a long laneway with a small section of wall remaining to the front of the laneway itself. This same lane shared access to a few other houses and a community club. To this day there are still thousands of wine and whiskey bottles left behind that same wall. They all belong to my dad.

The local shop was just a quarter of a mile away. This was a good walking distance for Dad. He enjoyed his walks. Many years earlier he had been fit. He had been a very good squash player. But that was all gone now. Now he always went out on the pretense of getting something, whether it was just for a breath of fresh air or to stretch the legs or simply for a pint of milk. I see now looking back that it didn't matter really as long as he got out. That was the important thing. He got out, and he got his fix.

I can visualize now what happened as Dad would arrive at our local shop. The owner, George, would see him entering the shop through the newly installed automatic doors. He would know exactly why he had come. George would then make a quick dive upstairs into the storeroom to grab a bottle or two of alcohol, any type, for my dad. It was the same routine day after day. George would then tuck the bottles quietly and discreetly into a brown paper bag and knowingly hand them over to my dad underneath the counter when no one was looking. He did it with such a lovely smile. You couldn't help but smile back. In reality everyone was looking. George knew it too, but he knew it best not to say or do anything.

In fact the whole of town knew Dad was an alcoholic by this point in time, and not just any alcoholic either—he was a rip-roaring one; one who fell in and out of taxis and cars; one who fell into ditches and didn't come out till someone pulled him out. He even fell into the snow one Christmas and didn't come out till my sister spotted him from the corner of her eye just in time as she nearly drove over him. He had made it home that night by taxi and had gotten as far as the back of the house. We found him face down unconscious in a few inches of snow. It was most likely he had unknowingly tripped over the step leading up to a paved path, which was level to the back door.

Every Christmas was to become a living nightmare. In the early days Dad would head into town to get a Christmas tree, a real one, on Mum's request. Mum didn't drive, so this left only Dad to carry out this yearly task. Sometimes he would manage to get the tree, but then it would be left in the trunk of his car while he headed into the pub. One of us would then come to the rescue, once Mum gave out. I remember that Christmas dinner was a time for Dad to undermine and slag our latest brother-in-law, Tony, who was by then married to my sister Joan. Tony was a softy, very emotional, and at times a little high-strung. His father too had been an alcoholic—tragically his father too had died young from heart failure related to drink.

This slagging (or sarcasm) I know can be done in style when there is normality before and after, but when there is just this kind of behavior and nothing else, it is hard to see the good in it. Tony would barely come through the door and Dad would find some derogative statement to throw at him. It was endless—continuing on till the middle of the night until such time as Dad would pass out and we would carry him up to bed. Tony never retaliated, and we never supported him. We just didn't know to; this kind of thing to us had become normal.

The job of buying the Christmas tree got later and later every year as Dad would be sent into town only to return without a Christmas tree in tow. In the end Dad couldn't even make it to the place where the Christmas trees were being sold as the first pub he saw was enough to distract him completely as even this small task became too much for him. The same would happen with the turkey. Over the years we all slowly took over. Christmas day itself would be one of a long wait for Dad, one that allowed him time to recover from the night before, long enough to join us for dinner and wine. Eventually that went by the wayside too; we began to just eat without him.

We handled all of this upheaval at the time by making light of it. At the time that's all we believed we could do. Never did it dawn on anyone in my family to seek external help; I guess we thought this was all the norm of growing up in the country. Rob knew earlier on too about my mum and dad and their ongoing need for drink. They would without my knowledge send him up to the local shop for drink whenever they were too drunk to go themselves. He never told me; I found out accidentally one day and duly reprimanded them. They would sulk and then in no time at all resume their normal drinking activities as soon as their cravings drove them to.

I see now as I look back on those years that I spent every living hour constantly worrying about my parents' well-being and safety throughout my youth. I'm pretty sure I took on the parent role. Maybe it had always been that way? I would come home and go directly to the fridge to examine inside it only to find the usual diet yogurt, a head of iceberg lettuce, and little else except the odd open bowl of bachelor's baked beans in the fridge. This was for Dad so that when he awoke from his drunken slumber in the middle of the night, this item of food in the fridge would usually be good cause enough him to stop and eat where otherwise his mind might never had registered a need to eat at all.

The fridge was located on route to his usual haunt for his fix, the hot press. The hot press also happened to be located next to the switch for the heat; hence the reason why this switch spent a lot of time on but never off. It was a good excuse and a way of getting to the drink, but often this little switch was forgotten once copious amounts of drink had been taken, leaving one legless and unable to switch anything off. At those times, I used to wake up in the middle of the night and do the rounds of checks needed to keep all safe and sound, including turning off a constant blaring television that might have exploded were it not for a few hours rest in the middle of the night. Mum and Dad's hearing was also impinged. Their sensitivities to ordinary day sounds and sensations were completely eroded.

Once the contents of the fridge were confirmed I would then pull back the curtains and open a few windows for ventilation before taking a walk down to the shop to buy some fresh food (everything went on a tab). I would return shortly thereafter, getting everything ready, and coax Mum and Dad to join me in a bite to eat. They would happily eat with me once food was offered along with a bottle or two of wine. When it was sunny outside I would organize a barbecue. Mum and Dad loved any excuse to drink, so a barbecue was always greeted with cheer. Dad would set up the table and the barbecue itself while Mum and I got the glasses, hot plates, and cutlery organized. Rob would go to the shop to get the food and wine. Hours later, after all was eaten, we would sit outside drinking and laughing. Mum and Dad would have the music blaring in the background. It was either this or their television in their bedroom, but something always had to be making a lot of noise around the house.

These evenings, like all other evenings, would start off well but would end in always the same vein. Mum would serenade Dad with her soft songs of lost or undying love, and when she wasn't looking, Dad would not-too-carefully sneak off to the pub for his last few with anyone or no one. Those days always ended sad with a drunken lonely mum and an even drunker but always merry dad. Only if you got in the way of him and his drink did he get aggressive; that was the only thing that got to him.

Mum showed her obvious discontent by continually drinking herself legless too. One evening I happened to be sitting on the couch beside Rob. My mum floated (barely upright) in past us without even seeing us. She was humming away to herself like she was deliriously happy (drunk). Rob and I continued watching television, saying nothing to each other.

Suddenly we heard a loud bang behind us. We quickly turned around. I thought something electrical had exploded, but it hadn't. It was my mum standing not too far away from us with her back to us, her head facing down stuck into a bag of crisps, and she was munching loudly and hurriedly. She was most likely starving given that she had a preference to drink over food. She was also a secret eater; she would not have done this had she known we were looking at her.

When she had finished devouring the packet of crisps, she again loudly tucked the bag in underneath some newspapers as if to hide it. She then continued in her drunken swagger to the hot press room—unaware that we were in the same room as her. I see now it is hard to respect someone who gets so drunk that they lose control of all of their senses. By this time I had little respect for my mother, only a deep-seeded anger that even I was mostly unaware of. It was to come out in other forms and other ways. It was to be displaced, every now and then, upon those who did truly love me.

Throughout this period Joe and Joan had married, leaving me feeling very much behind. My family had all gone their separate ways. I was having thoughts of doing the same, of marrying Rob, but I had this one worry that always got in the way of my happiness of this event taking place. That was to be my mum and dad attending this happy event of mine and turning the event into one of the more embarrassing days of my life. They were capable of it, not purposely so, as it was their addiction and not them that caused such unrelenting havoc. They were simply unaware of any circumstances or conditions that required control other than the need to control their drinking to a state of near constant drunkenness.

Dad had made incoherent speeches at all of my sisters' and brothers' weddings, ones where he laughed his way through but ones where no one else laughed nor understood a single word uttered from his dribbling mouth. We would look at each other in a knowing mortified way. There was no reasoning with him, and in the end one of us always took it upon ourselves to reprimand him like a child while another grabbed him by the arm and led him away. My sister Joan for this very reason had just immediate family to her wedding with relatives and friends invited in later. This to me was becoming an ever increasingly realistic option. My beautiful dreams of my wedding day were never about my wishes and me but around how best to manage Mum and Dad. This was never to change over the years.

Eventually, after many continuous years of this or that trauma day in day out, we as a family finally called a meeting over our concerns for Dad first and foremost but for Mum too. In our innocence we saw Dad as being the true alcoholic at that time. I guess he was the more obvious one. We saw Mum as a heavy drinker but one who possibly had the ability to stop at any time—maybe even more so if we could just get Dad to stop first. We decided to address the issue of Dad with Mum telling her of our worry for his ever-worsening drink problem. She said little. She just agreed, with the odd nod here and there. We then approached Dad and told him that we had a place for him in a rehabilitation clinic in Limerick as a way of getting him off the drink for good.

We were relieved when he agreed to attend for a week. We all attended the first meeting whereby you confront the alcoholic about his erratic behavior and absences, which we duly did. We all did except Mum, but nobody at the time noticed this. I have only reflected on this since as I see how detrimental she was to his ever truly dealing with his addiction. She too was obviously an alcoholic but a more secretive one. Only now do I see that there are different types of alcoholics; the stereotypical image we have of one lying permanently on the side of the street is the obvious one, yet they too had to start somewhere. They too most likely once had a family, a home, and a life before the drink took over and left them with nothing, not even their dignity.

Rob went to see my dad one day while he was in Limerick. I rang him after to see how he got on. He told me that Dad was in complete denial, though he didn't use exactly those words at the time. He did so by relaying a story where Dad pointed to others around him and said that they were not like him at all or vice versa—that they had come directly from the side of the street and that it was them who were alcoholics in the true sense of the word, not him. He couldn't see any similarities between him, a successful businessman to his mind, and one of a "down and out" living on the street, as he termed it. He couldn't see that we his children had been keeping him from the street. I'm not too sure we even saw this then.

He along with most people at the time couldn't see that he had stopped seeing reality—that the reality he had held in his mind even in treatment was of the old dad who once was, the successful one, not this other dad whom we had all come to know and remember with greater clarity. This one was the one who wet the bed most nights because he was too drunk to make it to the bathroom by himself. This trip to Limerick was followed in subsequent years by three trips to a local hospital (where he would be put to sleep for a week) and a further trip to Athy Addiction Recovery Centre. Unfortunately none of them worked.

Just as detrimental to Dad was Mum's reaction each and every time. It was to become obvious that she could not handle this new sober dad as she had been continuing in her secretive drinking in his absence. We didn't see this back then, but the result was that within a few days of his return I would see her disappear up to their bedroom with hot whiskies in hand, one for her and one for Dad. Before long he would be back on the drink heavier than ever before, and so would she.

As children of alcoholics we showed little obvious signs of any outward turmoil or pain at this time. However, there remained one exception to this, and that was my brother Tom, the eldest boy and by now the disinherited heir to the family fortune. He was continuing to show an ever-increasing liking for drugs over drink, something even my parents disapproved of. He was still young and beautiful but unfortunately very angry at the world. The promised inheritance was slowly disappearing. It was getting lost in drink.

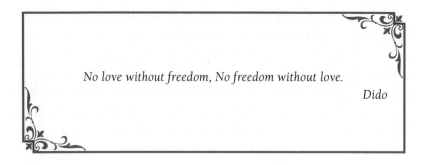

No love without freedom, No freedom without love.

Dido

CHAPTER 8

A Move to Waterford

I can remember that we discussed little of anything serious, Rob and I. We certainly didn't talk much of my family or of my mum and dad. We were young and carefree or at least were supposed to be, but I certainly wasn't. I just spent every spare minute I had with Rob. I had nothing else to do, nothing else to think about. I realize now that I clung to him. I clung to him so much so that if he wanted to go anywhere, which was rare, I went with him. If he wanted to go home to see his parents, I went with him. Wherever he went I went. I had nowhere else to go to.

I quickly began to suffocate whatever life had been in our relationship. Slowly and understandably it became boring and predictable. There was no room for creativity or trying anything new here; I simply couldn't handle it. So when Rob didn't tell me he was moving to Waterford (a two-hour drive away) until just the week before, I was furious and deeply hurt. He didn't react to my hurt. He calmly told me how he had gone as far as he could in his current role and that he needed to broaden his experience.

His friend Alex had recommended him to the company he was leaving; now he was moving on to another company as a new manager. He thought Rob would be the perfect replacement for himself. He was right—he was. So he got the job, accepted it, and moved all within the week. He bought flowers for my mum as a way of saying thanks for having kindly taken him in to her home. Just before Rob moved to Waterford he surprised me with the gift of a dog. He had heard about this farmer at work who had a few pups, sheepdogs. He wanted to get rid of them. Rob told his friend who knew the farmer that he had a home for one of them; that home was mine. I had always loved dogs.

So Rob brought it home with him that Friday evening before he was due to move on my return from college. We named him Ferrari. But looking back this probably wasn't a good name for a sheepdog without sheep to follow. Within six weeks of living with us, he got run over by a car passing our gateway at speed. My reaction was akin to having lost Rob himself. I was inconsolable. I was feeling left behind—giving me the dog confirmed this—and so when he died it was like mourning the end of a phase on our relationship. It was like a light went off—was this to be the end of us?

I chose to blame Rob for my insecurities. Instead of talking it through—I didn't know how to talk back then never mind feel—I concluded that he was abandoning me. I felt like I had lost control of the situation, and the only way I knew of getting it back was to tell Rob it was over. He in turn was devastated. I know now looking back that it must have been very lonely for him. It must have been traumatic for him, unlike his own upbringing. I didn't see the impact it was having on him at the time. I do now. Looking back I see that he was desperate to get away. He wasn't as it turns out looking to get away from me; he needed to get away from the chaos that was Mum and Dad. The thing was that he didn't know how to say that—nobody back then knew how to deal with alcoholism. So he simply went his way and I went mine and that was that.

That summer, in my third year of college, I worked in a large family-run retail store close to my home. They were a well-known company; their family knew of my family, and vice versa. At the time they saw my upset over my breakup with Rob. They felt sorry for me and mothered me, taking me out at night and giving me plenty of words of encouragement. It was a lovely experience.

But like everyone else they didn't see anything else. They didn't see that I was also devastated over my mum and dad both being alcoholics. They didn't see that my family as a whole was neglecting me. They didn't see that nobody really cared about what happened to me. I didn't tell them. I kept it all inside. I worked and did what I was told. I didn't know what else to do. I had run out of options. There was no one left to listen to me except Rob maybe.

Some weeks later, when my pride had recovered, I relented enough to focus my time on slowly coaxing Rob back in my life. For someone like me, with copious amount of determination, this wasn't a very hard thing to do. Eventually I was to move to Waterford too. It was becoming somewhat clear to me that even visiting home was becoming more and more of a nightmare. One evening, I returned home mid-week from college. It was just after Rob had made his move. I walked in to find the living room television blaring (usually it was the television in Mum and Dad's room that was constantly on at full volume) and Tom's drugs and drink everywhere. I knew he had made it home once again.

At the time my brother Tom was consumed with X-rated videos as well as all kinds of funny-looking drugs. I quickly became irate. He was always totally inconsiderate of anyone else in the room or house, and this occasion in particular was to be of little difference. I walked staunchly into Tom's room with a swagger akin to a parent about to take control and saw that he had female company. By now he had separated, so I had no issue with him having company, I had an issue with the manner in which it was being carried out.

I closed the door quickly behind me and fled into Mum and Dad's room only to find that they too had their television up at full volume (usually the news) and they were spaced out in the bed with drink. It was obvious that they had not heard a thing. I then continued on down the corridor, just like a detective at work, to discover another couple in the end room also making out. By now I was past being irate; I was just consumed with a rightful rage at the disrespectfulness of my brother's Tom's actions.

This time I didn't move. I stood my legs wide and fixed to the ground and told the couple unknown to me in no uncertain terms to get out of our family home this instant. I stood there harassing them until they dressed in front of me and left. By now Tom on hearing the commotion got dressed too and met me at his door leading onto the hallway.

I turned viciously toward him, demanding that he too leave. He didn't, so I threatened him to within an inch of his life (verbally). He knew deep down that I was not going to be calmed. I think he also knew that he was in the wrong. He was a good person underneath, but like us all he was lost. He like us all had been given little support and no clear direction on anything.

Tom moved out that night and didn't come back inside Mum and Dad's house till many years later. He took up home with the lady he had met that night. Things calmed down at home for a while with just me and Mum and Dad and their heavy drinking sessions. It was all the stability I needed to get me to my end of term in college, where I received an honors degree in human resources management. I took it as a sign that it was the end of an era and time for me to move on in life to bigger and better things. I left my failed self behind for a time.

*   *   *

Directly after college I took up a graduate vacancy with a pharmaceutical firm based in Waterford. It was the first day in July 1997 when I started in their Human Resources Division. At the time I kept as much as I could to myself. I worked, got by, and hid behind Rob. He worked long hours and was a hard worker, just like my dad had been in his youth. He would head to work early and come home late with Saturday slowly becoming a part of his normal working week. I had nothing else to do but walk and read, so that's what I did in between more studies, this time a degree in MRP (don't ask me why material planning; I think it was just the In thing to do at the time).

From the start, I did better in my job than I ever thought I would, given my upbringing. My determination for a "normal" life was driving me to success, and successful I slowly became. I still had a little bit of unpredictability or quick temperedness in me, and one never knew when this would flair up; but maybe those in work saw this as very much a part of being an extremely focused individual. Maybe they thought a little bit of unpredictability was worth putting up with given my ability to maintain and exceed the ever-increasing personal targets put before me.

By now Rob and I had moved into together into a one-bedroom apartment. It was close to the city, so much so that I began walking in and out to work every day. I can still remember every inch of our first apartment together, where we made some of the happiest memories I have of that time. I had brought a beautiful blue bedspread from home and used it on our double bed. I spent the first week scrubbing everything and anything, and when Rob arrived home that Friday evening for the weekend, I led him proudly into our first bedroom of our own making. He was thrilled too. That weekend was special; it was my first taste of true freedom.

Unfortunately it was not to last too long. I had a raging anger underneath always waiting to come up to the surface. Within a year of the move to Waterford, Rob's friends started to marry one by one, leaving just us left. I hadn't stayed in contact with any of mine, so I had few if any friends. I didn't know how to stay in contact. Back then it wasn't as easy either. The Internet and mobile phones were only starting to come into use along with the ability of our young to find employment locally or nationally without fear of having to emigrate.

I started to put Rob under pressure for us to marry. He was more than happy; it was just a matter of funds, so I took on this responsibility in earnest. I took money from him every month and started to put a wedding and holiday fund in place. The interesting thing was that by now Rob had been working for four years, and yet after twelve months, I was making double his money. I was receiving positive feedback on my performance, and subsequently my job role expanded, as did my salary.

I was becoming frustrated with Rob's lack of financial progress or obvious progression in life itself. He was happy for things to remain the same forever more. I on the other hand only looked forward to my two weeks of holidays a year, but this was becoming less and less of compensation as time wore on. I knew deep down that I was searching for more than just staying at the same level for the rest of my life. Either way, whether promoted or not, Rob was happy. This was beginning to cause friction between us. The honeymoon of living together in the early days was wearing off, and I was left having no idea what I was going to do next. All I knew was that I had to do something. It was gnawing away at my insides.

I began to get angry with Rob. I started to take out all my frustrations on him. I remember clearly when my anger climaxed. It was at a wedding in Kerry. Rob's cousin was getting married, and the night before the wedding they had a party in their house. A friend of the girl getting married took an obvious fancy to Rob, and he looked to enjoy it a little too much. I said little. I just sat back seething, drinking myself more jealous as the night unfolded.

In the privacy of our bed later, I let go of every piece of anger I had held inside. I exploded upon Rob, kicking and screaming. I punched and kicked him all the way to the floor, where I followed him and punched some more. I completely lost it. Rob as always did little. He just got up, got back into bed and pretended to sleep. Eventually my anger subsided and I too fell asleep beside him. The next morning, Rob kindly suggested I "try to get some counseling." I never did. Neither of us every brought this incident up again, but it forever shook me. Everything about my anger terrified me.

As I look back, I realize only now that it was at this stage in my life that my sisters casually revealed to me that Dan had abused both my sister Joan and my cousin, Aunt Bridget's daughter. It was then that the penny finally dropped as to why Aunt Bridget reacted the way she did to me the day I decided to run away to Dan's house. It also explained why my sister Joan had become obese almost overnight. While we all experienced weight gain (and losses) over the years, as a family not one of us was ever close to being obese. She told me many years later that she did it to make sure no one found her attractive enough to abuse again.

I did at this time open up to Rob about my childhood abuse, but like with my parents' alcoholism, he didn't know what to do in response. He again suggested that I get some counseling while never bringing my abused past up again for discussion. He was dealing with it in the same way that my family was, and it's only now that I see that this was the final straw.

While I had consistent and kind love with Rob, that in itself was no longer enough; I wanted and needed more. I wanted someone I could talk with, someone who could communicate with me on my level, someone who could see the torment I was in and possibly help me through it. I was also searching to make reality of my dreams—a dream of growing and becoming more than my past had given to me. Somewhere along the line, I had made a promise to myself to never give up on my dreams. I wanted it all—true happiness, fun, and love—and nothing was going to stop me.

Eventually, after two years of our living together, I found the words to tell him that I was unhappy. I was unhappy with us. It was a Saturday afternoon. It was sunny outside, and we were cooped up inside a cold, damp one-bedroom apartment watching Indie race driving. Rob was addicted to it. He was also addicted to reading his bike and car magazines. He was beginning to get addicted it seemed to anything else but me.

I was not too sure he heard me, so I left. I went outside and walked. The fresh air was lovely. I was at peace again. It brought me back to when I was a child running up and down the hills at home. It brought me back to a moment in time when I was happiest, on my own in nature surrounded by sheer beauty.

When I returned I repeated what I had said to him early: "I'm unhappy, Rob."

He said nothing. He didn't know what to say. I started to cry. He was by now reading his car magazine. I lay down beside him on the couch and pulled his arm around me and snuggled into him. He responded by rubbing my arm and giving me a kiss on the forehead. He then went back to his reading. I cried quietly so as not to disturb him.

A few weeks later I decided that it was time to have a more serious chat with Rob about us. I arranged for us to go for dinner locally. I had tied it in with my completion of my MRP qualification, which I gained part time, and so it was also to be a celebration of that. We sat across from each other surrounded by lots of laughter and chat. We were in the corner of a pub. It was renowned for its food and liveliness. I ordered a glass of wine. I was relaxing after all the endless hours studying. I decided to sit back and observe for a while. I decided not to say anything for a while.

I looked across at Rob. He looked at me and smiled. He was happy, I could tell. He was happy, relaxing away, not a care in the world. He used to say to me, "I could die now I'm so happy. I'm ready to die anytime." For him this meant he had everything he wanted, right there at the moment in time. It couldn't get any better, he would say. We said very little to each other through the dinner. In fact we barely uttered a word to each other. I thought of his mum and dad and how they did the same. How they used to sit side by side day in and day out and say nothing to each other. We were just like that, Rob and me, and for Rob that was okay. That was more than okay. That was everything he wanted.

This was the ever-growing gap between us of what we wanted out of life. I began to have these little chats with myself: *If we get married, do you think you could do this forever? Is this really what life has to offer?* My reply was, *I'm not sure, but something tells me I will end up having an affair. I'm afraid I won't remain faithful to him.* Those thoughts scared me. I knew I didn't want that for him or for me. I knew we both deserved more.

Shortly after that Rob and I separated. It was coming up to Christmas. I suggested that we both go to our own families for Christmas, that I would then come back early and move my stuff so that by the time he came back to work in the new year, I would be gone. I wanted to cause a little fuss as possible. I remember that around this time we slept with our backs to each other. One night Rob turned around and we made love; it was desperately passionate. Then we both turned our backs to each again and slept. Neither said anything. That was to be our ending, a kind love with no words.

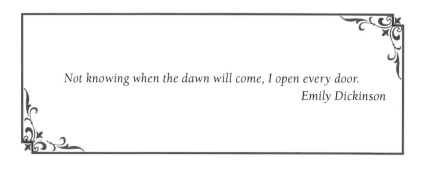

Not knowing when the dawn will come, I open every door.
Emily Dickinson

CHAPTER 9

A Fresh Start

*F*rom the moment when I met Eoin our relationship was intense. Everything about both of us was intense. It started off with a phone call, me to him. He was looking for work. He had e-mailed me his curriculum vitae for a vacancy in our Waterford plant. I rang him. My conversation started off the same way as it always did: "Hi my name is Jean. I'm calling from a company called Merrill Pharmaceutical. Can you talk at the moment?" He laughed. I said nothing. I thought maybe there was something wrong with the phone line. I pressed my ear closely to the phone. I was in business mode. He laughed again.

"Shhhh," he said. "Quiet down, lads, I'm talking to the secret service. Quiet. Quiet." He chuckled. "Hello. Hello. Who's this again?" he said. He told me many months later that he had been out the night before with a few friends of his and had been asleep on one of their bedroom floors when I rang. I remember thinking he was funny. He had that dry sense of humor just like my dad. I had it too when I wanted it; but this was work, and in work I didn't. In work I was deadly serious. I was going places, and there could be no messing about.

I continued in my business tone. I explained who I was and why I was calling and again asked if it was a good time for him to talk. He said jovially, "It is." I told him about the position I had in mind for him. I asked him to tell me about his last role, why he was looking to move, what he was really looking for. He laughed again. "What am I really looking for?" He paused as if pensive, as if stuck in serious thought. He then said, "Well, whatever it is, Jean. It is Jean, isn't it?"

I replied, "Yes, it is Jean."

He continued, "Well, whatever it is, Jean, you have it." He paused for a moment and then said, "Yes, I'm pretty sure you have what I'm looking for." His voice echoed confidence. It was deliberate, articulate, and funny. Just what I didn't realize I needed.

Our conversations continued like this for many weeks. I felt safe. I felt excited. My relationship with Rob had just come to an end. This felt good. These conversations gave me something to look forward to. I remember that he always managed to call me at a good time. I was sharing an office with my new boss, as I had been promoted again; if possible she was even more serious than me, so there was little time for chitchat. That's why she liked me so much. She was older than me, but we got on well because I didn't do chitchat; I worked.

Our conversations got longer and longer each time he'd call. I used to laughingly tell him that he could talk for Ireland. He said his mother said the same. Then one day out of the blue he stopped calling. Three weeks passed before I heard from him again. I was quite annoyed when he did finally ring, and my conversation started with "I was worried about you. In fact I was very worried about you. Are you okay?" I hadn't thought to call him. I don't know why.

I just knew in that moment that I hadn't stopped thinking about him. He said casually, "I was in hospital there for a while. I'm okay now. Everything is fine."

I asked, "What were you in hospital for?"

He replied, "It's a long story."

We talked for some time. He told me that he had fainted one day while at home in his mum and dad's house. It was out of the blue, unexpected, and his parents had insisted that he get himself fully checked. They were concerned about him too.

He said he was okay now. "The good news, Jean, is that I am as fit as a fiddle. There is not a single thing wrong with me anywhere." He had done every test in the medical book including a brain (CAT) scan, and the good news was that all was well. He was in his mid-thirties. He had been a sports star in his youth, so in hindsight the testing was probably a good idea. He had a few scars, he said, but nothing to worry about. He made light of it. I knew it wasn't for me to probe too much more, so I left it at that. I told him about my boring life.

From there on, my conservations with Eoin became a daily feature. Although I hadn't placed him, as of yet, it was obvious that we were becoming close. I had just moved into a new apartment along Main Street with a new friend from work. The first thing I did was buy a fabulous new state-of-the-art music system and a set of tailor-made curtains—the only two things my room was missing. I then went about ordering a new car, an Alfa Romeo. Things were going well at work, so happily I could afford to buy whatever I wanted. At last I had arrived in the land of financial stability.

By March of 2000 I had begun dating Eoin. We had arranged a blind date a few weeks earlier. I had plucked up the courage to ask him to come up to Waterford for a night so that we could meet for the first time in person. He agreed, and it was a fun night to remember. He was extremely talkative, outgoing, and charismatic. He also had a love of the outdoors just like me. We spent many hours in our early times together walking hand in hand while chatting aimlessly about all sort of interesting things—love, feelings, values, sport. It wasn't long before we fell madly in love.

From the very beginning I opened up to Eoin about my abused past. He was more than happy to discuss my turbulent history with me. He referred to my troubled childhood as my demons—but he did so in a kind and understanding way. He never offered any solution per se, but he did allocate blame squarely on my family's shoulders. He thought they were very unsupportive of me. This had an immediate effect on Eoin's relationship with my family. Neither party ever warmed to the other.

Shortly after this Eoin was offered a role in our Waterford plant, and as part of the initial training, he was required to move to Massachusetts for a period of six months, which he duly did. This put our relationship under strain given that we only got to see each other twice in this period, but nevertheless we stayed in contact, with me rushing home each day for his daily phone call. Within weeks of us dating Eoin had told me of some sad story relating to his finances, and given that I had some extra cash in the bank at the time with little else to do with it, I gave a few thousand to him. I thought nothing of it; I just saw that I was helping a friend out.

By this time, my eldest sister Angela had just finalized her divorce. She had divorced well, if there is such a thing. I thought her lucky to have been married; I was as of yet still unmarried. She agreed to go halves with me on a house in a prime location in Waterford. House prices in Ireland had skyrocketed by this time so much so many first-time buyers like me couldn't get on the property ladder. The only way to do it was to go halves with someone else. It was a good investment piece for both of us, and so I took this time to have fun furnishing it and doing it up as nice as possible, as it was my intention to live there.

I moved in, and Eoin joined me shortly after his return from Massachusetts. It was difficult from the beginning, as Eoin did not have money to pay rent and so it was then up to me to both pay my mortgage and pay my sister her half in rent. But in no time at all Eoin convinced me not to pay my sister rent, and so I just stopped without discussing it with her, a decision I have since lived to regret, as simply put it was the wrong decision.

Without knowing it, the stress of my new relationship (the excitement of it blinding me to his lack of support) and my lack of family connection was getting to me. Again Eoin had me convinced that it was down solely to my family. He observed how they never rang me (his parents rang him every day), and if anyone did ring me it was usually just my rich sister looking for the money I owed her. Not one of them came willingly to visit. Maybe they saw me as being miserable, which was probably the case at the time. All my focus and money went to the new house or Eoin—I had none left for anyone else!

I began to get restless and disheartened with both my work and home life. Work had become routine, and for someone like me who likes variety, it wasn't enough for me anymore. Eoin had a job but never had money to do anything and always seemed to be working late. So instead of confronting all my obvious issues, I hatched a plan to escape. I was close to a breaking point; I just didn't know it.

I nervously gave notice to my employers in early 2001. I decided to take time out to go to Canada to visit my sister Maria; she had returned to her husband some years earlier. Eoin was very supportive of my move to Canada; he had been there a few years earlier and had loved it. The difference was that he had family and financial support and I had none. Before I left again Eoin convinced me to get a ten thousand Irish pounds loan from a local bank in order to cover the mortgage while I was away. He was to remain in my house for safekeeping sake. Somehow he made it all make sense, and so I agreed and left with both my car and my house in his hands.

I arrived in Canada with little money of my own by this point. The house move and Eoin's ongoing lack of financial support left me with little personally. My sister Angela gave me three hundred Irish pounds to get me by. I arrived to a then-broke sister in Canada. She and her husband had invested in their early-married life in shares that the government later taxed. They spent years paying off the tax, a young couple with two young children.

So it was important to hit the ground running, which I did. Having grown up with financial insecurity all my life and with no thought of how best to protect myself, I was anxious to get the money rolling in. I knew that I only had myself to rely on and no one else, so I quickly secured two jobs, working by day in a pub and by night in a restaurant next door to the pub. I possibly could have looked for more appropriate work to that of my experience, but I didn't. I think maybe I didn't have the confidence to. I didn't think I was good enough; I had been lucky in Waterford to secure a role as a senior human resources specialist, but for whatever reason I didn't feel as lucky or as confident in Canada.

While my sister Maria was lovely to me throughout this time, she only had eyes for her now husband, and all her thoughts and actions surrounded him and little else. From the outside she was like my mother; she was allowing someone else to do the thinking for her. Her husband worked shift (nine days offshore followed by five days home leave), so when he wasn't around, I along with her two sons got the pleasure of her company. But when her husband was around and available, we all got dropped in preference for his needs. His likes and dislikes came first; it just so happened that he was more a bachelor type who was more interested in cars and motorbikes than family life, but Maria, like my mother, didn't let this impact her love of him in any way.

Unknown to me I was doing exactly the same thing with Eoin. I was only happy when I was putting his happiness before me. It would be a long time before I started to see my connection to my sisters and parents and vice versa and how we were all had exactly the same vices; they just played out in many different ways. As a result the whole time in Canada was a lonely experience for me. I met some gorgeous, considerate, and kind people. But I was incapable of opening up to them. I wasn't capable of being normal.

I was hard-working and easy company in many respects, but I was aloof, quiet, and thoughtful. I found it hard to receive compliments. I found it hard to accept kindness, and on the inside I was finding it hard to fit in. In fact, I was plain miserable. I just never told anyone. I kept hoping someone from home would call me to see if I was okay, to see if I was still alive. But they didn't. They were too busy being miserable like me, and like me they simply didn't realize it.

One of my more upsetting memories was of my sister Maria ringing home every week to a muted response. It changed my own approach to her calls in later years. I knew from being on the other side of the phone, the home side, that when she rang my mother and sisters would raise their eyes to heaven and say, "Oh no, it's Maria again, Miss Chatterbox." Mum in particular would find this call a terrible inconvenience. We would take turns taking or avoiding her call as it were. We were busy people, you see. We had things to do and didn't have time to be talking to Maria, who was calling all the way from Canada.

I would idly observe my mother as she snoozed, seated quietly and cradling the phone on her neck. She would give the odd "Mmm … yeah, yeah … mm mm" before snoozing again; the drink from Sunday dinner was making her wish she could just sleep. Maria used to do all the talking. She had no choice; there was little coming her way in return. But she was well used to that even if she wasn't aware that she was.

We would all know when the end would come as Mum would say, "Everything fine here; nothing to report," and quickly say her good-byes with a "love to all" before hanging up and reaching for the rest of her drink. She now needed one; you could tell by the look on her face that she was now exhausted and needed another drink to re-relax her. This was Mum to a tee; instead of being excited to hear from her daughter, she was dismissive. She lacked any respect for her daughter's efforts to stay in contact with home; she lacked any interest in her or her life.

I went to Canada in February 2001, and by October I had had enough. I wanted out; I missed home. I was terribly unhappy. I tried not to show it to my sister, but even if I did, I'm sure she wouldn't have known what to do. Nobody in my family did. So I did the best thing that I could have done at the time: I returned home. It happened to tie in with September 11 when there was worldwide panic and mayhem over flights and was just at the tail end of Eoin's brief visit with me, so I used it as an excuse to leave. I used everything as an excuse to leave as long as it wasn't me.

Eoin and I traveled back home separately. We met up back at my house in Waterford, where I reclaimed my car. We continued to share the house, and I continued paying all the bills. By this time, his job in Waterford had come to an end, as the country was entering a deep recession. I was a little panicky as money was drying up. So I did the only thing I could think of doing, which was to casually make contact with my previous employer. She was excited to hear from me. This was a surprise to me, as very few people up to this point were excited to hear from me. I had always felt like a nuisance to my parents and family generally.

My boss asked me to come see her; she had an opening for me elsewhere. I called the following day, and she told me of an opportunity at a senior level in Kilkenny, an hour away from Waterford. She arranged for me to meet the Kilkenny team the very next day. I traveled early the following morning, spent the day with the team, and liked what I saw. I returned to Waterford and agreed to move with Eoin, and that was that. I took the job and we set about moving.

Eoin organized renting out the house in Waterford, and as the house was bare—being new—I had to buy a few pieces of furniture. This left things very tight with the rent just covered the mortgage. I rented an apartment in Kilkenny close to work and started the following week, as we needed the money. I was excited; I knew I could do this job in my sleep. Shortly after our move, my sister called me. She wanted me to sell the house. She was naturally unhappy that she was still not getting any return from her investment. I grudgingly agreed to put the house up for sale. We were lucky, as the property was in a good location and so was easily sold at a small profit for us both.

At the same time, events around Eoin's finances were unfolding. It turned out that while in his first job he had traded in shares and lost, lost a lot. I think it was some forty thousand or so in one loan. It's hard for me now to remember the details—I have blotted them out—but I think there were a couple of other small loans too, so he told me, to the value of ten thousand or more.

With this in mind, I thought I needed more money, so I convinced my reluctant sister to give me an extra ten thousand from the sale of the house than was due to me in our 50/50 agreement. This naturally led to us not talking for years. It was probably not a bad thing in hindsight. I didn't think she was a very nice person at the time, and I'm pretty sure as I look back that she most likely felt exactly the same way about me.

So here I was with over forty thousand in the bank, a ten thousand bank loan of my own, and a new job all in Kilkenny. I was doing well by anybody's standards, and instead of having the strength to protect myself or even pay off my own loan, I did what all damaged adults do—I put Eoin's issues before my own and gave him the majority of my money to pay off his "stock/gambling" loans. At the time I thought money was easy made. I was planning our future. I was making sure there were no obstacles in his way to marrying me. He was debt free now; we were going to get through this. I fixed the problem, or so I thought.

I worked hard. I worked day and night, weekends, and even Sundays. Eoin was looking for a job but couldn't find one. I was doing so well that shortly thereafter I was promoted to manager. I work harder, and still Eoin couldn't get a job. I couldn't get him a job, or so he told me, so now that was my problem too. Still it didn't dawn on me. I loved him. Everything was okay; I was beginning to rake it in again.

Shortly after this, I won an award for my contribution to the company. Work-wise I was on top of my game. I was even making a friend in work. Geraldine was her name. We were a great team. I had guts and determination; she was sweet and lovely, and everyone loved her. I overhauled and restructured many of the archaic systems, while she worked behind the scenes to get everyone's "buy in." We were invincible—for a time.

But even this friendship in the end was to turn sour, as I overpowered her, and she in turn threw draggers—of jealousy—into my back. It was survival of the fittest. Geraldine ended up leaving, but we talked again years later, and I knew that she had forgiven me and I had forgiven her for any nastiness that had taken place between us. It was obvious looking back that we were victims of circumstance. It was obvious to me after that I would never go back to being that "unhealthily competitive" person ever again.

Hold fast to dreams,
For if dreams die
Life is a broken-winged bird
That cannot fly.

Langston Hughes

CHAPTER 10

A Birth

One weekend in early 2003 I was heading home in my little sporty Alfa Romeo when I crashed into the back of a Jeep. I wrote off my car, my gorgeous car, my little piece of freedom— one of the few things in life that was mine, all mine. An experienced local policeman came to my rescue. He told me how lucky I was. As we followed my car being towed to a crash repair yard, he pointed to various bends along with way where parents had lost young adults. He knew them all by name and age. He knew where they all had lived. It was a reminder to me of how lucky I was to have survived such tragedy. That day I did feel lucky to have survived.

I searched my car for my phone. It was in the back underneath the rubble. I remember looking down at my jumper. It was ruined from the airbag. Dust was everywhere on me and on the car, and there was a small rip in my jumper where I had collided with the driving wheel. I was upset, as the purple jumper had been a gift from Eoin. He had just bought it for me that Christmas.

I rang Eoin. He was back in Kilkenny, meeting up with his best friend Gerry. I was going home to give him our apartment for the weekend. He canceled his weekend with Gerry, a wee bit unhappy, as at this point he was feeling my clinginess. He collected me and brought me back to the apartment. Toward the end of the weekend, he went home. Something had come up; it always did.

I was still very shaken, so I rang Geraldine first thing Monday to let her know that I wouldn't be in. She understood. She rang me later that day and instantly on hearing the pain and shock in my voice, she dropped everything and came to my rescue. She picked up chips and chicken along with way and stayed and chatted with me for the night. I was so very grateful. Nobody from home rang me even after I rang them to let them know I was still alive.

Eoin convinced me to give him more money; he would give me money back each month. He did the first two months and then stopped. I was getting tired of the situation, so one day after confronting him calmly we agreed that he should move home with his parents. I then set about renting a house with a few other girls. Eoin and I agreed that we would see each other on weekends. He was happy; he felt lonely waiting around all day for me to come home from a long day's work.

I moved into a small house close to work with a girl called Carol, and at first it worked. Things got easier. I had work during the week and Eoin on weekends. I started to go to the gym every night. I started to eat healthier. I took up yoga, first at class and then at home. I loved it. I found that it relaxed me. My housemate was generally unhappy that I had a boyfriend down with me most weekends. She felt that her space was not her own anymore—it was after all her house.

For some reason Eoin was slow to bring me to his house. His mum and dad were full-time supporting his sister, Shauna, and her child Sean. They had enough going on, he told me, as in addition his mother's sister was dying of cancer, a long slow painful death. She liked the house to be kept quiet when she visited. I remember that one lucky occasion when I got invited to stay was at Sean's communion.

Eoin and I had been going out with each other for three years or so. I was invited to come, but only after Sean's communion Mass and subsequent family photos had been taken. The event started at twelve noon. I was allowed to attend from 4:00 p.m. onward along with all the other guests and only after Eoin's family's return to their house. I duly arrived feeling a little left out, but then I had always felt that, so was this occasion really in any way different? I remember at the time my sister Liz used to tease me, saying, "Are you sure he's not already married?" She was convinced that he was.

Shortly after this I found out that I was pregnant—at twenty-nine years of age it was a surprise. I had gone to work one day not feeling well. At the time it had never occurred to me not to go to work if I was unwell. But as the day progressed I got more and more sick. I decided to call to my GP shortly after lunch. She asked me if I thought I might be pregnant. I replied, "No way." It hadn't even occurred to me. I took the pregnancy test. Once completed, she casually told me, "Well, you're pregnant!" I cried out of shock. I stumbled out of her office and went to my car and did the only thing I could think of doing at the time—I called Eoin.

He was obviously in shock too as he asked me, "Is the child mine?"

I said, "Yes, of course it is."

I cried some more. What was wrong with me? It must be my hormones. I thought I was losing it! Eoin rang back later and apologized. The pregnancy had come at the wrong time he said. He was unprepared.

The following weekend, we agreed to tell Eoin's family that I was expecting. As we told them I could see the shock on all their faces. They hadn't been expecting this. They were only getting to know me. Tara, Eoin's mum, had acted anxious for the rest of the day. Eventually I calmly said, "Everything is going to be okay, Tara. It will work itself out."

She responded, "But I am worried, Jean. Eoin doesn't have a job. What will you do for money? Who will support the baby?"

I replied simply, "It's okay, Tara. I will. I have a good job. I'm a manager with a good salary. I will take care of everything."

The weekend after that I went home alone. Again I woke up the following morning crying. This time my mum heard me and entered the room. I think maybe she was expecting my news, because when I broke down and told her I was pregnant, she turned to me and said, "Everything will be fine, Jean. I'm delighted for you." It was a miracle! My mother actually acted like my mother for a time. I guess in this situation she really didn't have to worry too much. By then I was nearly thirty, and in all ways I was completely independent of her.

I remember being very sick for the first five months of my pregnancy, so much so that I initially lost weight; then my weight leveled off some. I used to leave work for an hour every day at lunchtime and just go back to my rented room and sleep. The sleep was bliss. I was cranky at work during those initial few months. If anyone cooked anything, I smelled it a mile away and subsequently had to run to the bathroom to vomit.

One weekend, just as I was getting back to normal, I returned home to Cork to visit my sister Liz and her family. I was just six months pregnant. By now I was back to the weight I was supposed to be for this stage of pregnancy. As I entered her back kitchen door Liz commenced singing, "Jean got fat. Jean got fat," to which her children and husband joined in. I was shocked, but as per usual I said nothing. She then hugged me, smiled, and turned back into the nice Liz. This was Liz to a tee, one minute motherly and sweet, the next sarcastic and bitchy.

My pregnancy, as it turns out, was a fabulous time of my life. I started to look after myself just a little bit better. I gave myself permission to, after all I had to—there was someone else inside me to consider now, and it wasn't just my body anymore. I ate healthy organic food only, certainly no wine or cigarettes, and switched to organic noncarcinogenic body products including shampoo and conditioner. I even stopped dying my hair. I did yoga daily and took long slow walks in the evening, happily chatting away to my little unborn child. I planned to be the best mum in the world. I looked forward to our summer together when I would have time off work. At last, I had something of my very own to focus all my attention and love on.

At this time, my housemate and the house owner decided to move to the States. She gave me a few months notice to leave her accommodation. I knew that I had to find a place to live and quickly. My newfound friend Adele helped me. I had met her through work. She was artistic by nature. I knew that she had vision and would help me find my new home. I spotted a two-bed apartment with a lovely sea view. She agreed with me—this was the place for me. Shortly after this, I suggested that Eoin move back in with me in time for the birth of the baby. He agreed. Till then, I had lots to organize and sort out.

My heart was set, so I went about getting a mortgage. I was lucky. I had no loans—I had just completed paying them off—and no money in the bank, but I had a good salary. I got the mortgage I was looking for with ease, but the apartment was not to be ready till just before my due date. In the meantime, my friend Adele kindly invited me into her small cozy house with her three children. She cooked for me daily and gave me lots of space, and all in all we had three fabulous months of fun together before the day arrived for me to finally move into my very own new home.

Around this time, I panicked that I wasn't married. Partly it had to do with my upbringing, but I also felt that it had to do with the society in which I grew up. In the early stages of my pregnancy I had bled a lot, so much so that I had nearly lost my baby. I met many nurses on my many trips to the hospital, as around this time I had to go to the hospital for daily checkups where I would be scanned to see if the baby was still alive. I remember one nurse suggesting that it might be a good thing if I were to lose the baby. I knew the inference was due to the fact that I was unmarried; I had just completed the form where this information was included along with my religious status. But despite all my little unborn and I held our own.

I wanted to be married so badly that one weekend I harassed Eoin when I was up in his family home. I told him I wasn't going back to work without an engagement. He agreed but said he had no money. He was still unemployed. I had money, so I suggested that I buy the ring; and that's what I did. Within a month, I had a beautiful ring and my wedding planned—for a year after our baby was born. As expected, we decided that a quiet wedding was best, minimizing the impact of Mum and Dad's sure-to-be-drunken state. As many of my work colleagues were also planning their marriages, I readily had information on venues, photographers, bands, and hairdressers available to me. Given my organized nature, I just went ahead and booked them within the week of our engagement. All that was needed was a dress, but I knew that was going to be easy, as I was a perfect size ten, having learned from Eoin that exercise was the only way to get me there.

At this point, I choose to opt for the public—no cost attached—health services as opposed to private. Being "public" in Ireland means that you have all the services of a private plan but that you join the largest waiting lists for all hospital procedures. The only other thing was that on admission to hospital you are assigned a cubicle in a very large room as opposed to a private room. But this didn't bother me, nor did I feel that I was jeopardizing my health in any way, as I saw myself as very fit and healthy at this point. Up to this point, I had been going to the gym five days a week alongside a daily yoga routine. I was a walker and a nondrinker. What could go wrong?

Going private was a very expensive option, and I was more interested in focusing my money on getting ready for our baby. Usually this meant that you are given minimum access to a gynecologist, because consultants such as these are expensive. For some reason, though, the gynecologist assigned to me always happened to be around when my routine hospital scan was due. I guess I was lucky, because this was highly unusual if not unknown.

During a routine scan at six months my gynecologist observed that the fluid around my baby was down a little from what was considered normal. As a result, I was admitted to the hospital for a week's rest. He then took time to check up on me twice daily while I rested in the hospital for the week. I could see that he was kind; I see now that he saw that I was very hard on myself, so much so that I'm pretty sure he made me rest.

After a week, I insisted on being let out; after all I had a two-bedroom apartment to move my bags of stuff into. He let me go but insisted that I take it easy and not lift anything. I ignored him, and on my release, I immediately went to move my many bags of stuff all on my own. No Eoin in sight. I had asked him to come down to help, but for whatever reason he simply couldn't at the time. I didn't take it personally; I just got on with getting ready for my baby.

I loved my new apartment. It was glorious to have a place to call home once again. My boss had given me a big bonus; I was doing a great job. I spent every penny on the apartment. Eoin moved back in with me two weeks before the baby was due. I worked until the Friday before my baby's due date. As my fluids never returned to normal, thereby preventing my baby from being able to turn itself and be delivered naturally, it was arranged for me to have a cesarean the following Monday, May 24, 2004.

Without thinking about anything too much, I calmly arrived for check in on the Monday morning promptly and as requested at 9:10 a.m., thirty minutes before the planned operation. By 9:40 a.m.—as there was no queue—I had a baby in my arms, a beautiful baby girl! It was quite a peculiarly easy experience in one sense, as I clearly remember turning fifteen with terrifying thoughts of natural childbirth in the forefront of my mind. Little did I know that those thoughts had been so unnecessary—the story of my life—always focusing or worrying about the wrong things.

I wasn't sure what to do with my first baby, so I read a few books on the subject. One book my sister Angela later referred to as *Mrs. Hitler's Baby Book*. She probably wasn't too far wrong. It was my holy grail. If Christine cried I looked it up. If she turned a week older, I looked it up. If I wasn't sure what she should be doing in her daily routine, I looked it up. I followed every recipe in the book to a tee. I even put up blacked-out curtains on her window and carried a travel set pair of blacked-out curtains for fear that Christine would wake up before it said to in the book. I can now honestly say looking back that I hadn't got a clue and obviously no one to show me.

Christine slept well at night from early on. She had even managed to sleep through on her very first night in this new world of hers, all six pounds, nine ounces of her. The duty nurse schooled me the following morning for letting her sleep through. What a selfish thing for me to do! It turned out, though, that Christine was a good eater from the very beginning. She also loved attention. She would simply scream insistently for it, but once you gave it to her, she was as happy as could be. She was active, bright, and full of expectations. She was truly a joy to watch, amid what was now a very depressing time in my life.

In the days after Christine was born, my sister Angela took a day trip down to see me while I was still in the hospital. She clearly didn't notice anything wrong with me or how lonely I was in a room all on my own. As I had gone public, which usually meant sharing with lots of other people in a large ward, it was unusual to have a room to your own. I managed to get one, but not because I asked for it; I just had that look of self-sufficiency. I had the ability to give off that aura of false confidence. The nurses put me into a room on my own, small and dingy with no TV, because they instinctively knew I could cope with anything and while everyone else had family, friends, and nurses rushing to their rescue, I stood alone. Few came to visit me besides my friend Adele, Eoin's parents, and Angela.

Eoin's parents arrived three days after Christine was born. They arrived to my tears and put it down to the "three-day blues." Instead of staying with me, they swiftly left after ten minutes, and once more I was left on my own. Eoin was in the throes of his addiction to his PC and online trading, so he would always venture in exhausted and leave me with feeling worse than before he came.

When I came home from the hospital with Christine, my sister Liz arrived on another quick drop-in day trip. No one wanted to hang around, I guess. She took one look at me and took over. She told me to eat—she instantly cooked a big greasy fry-up—that it was what I needed, that as always I was too skinny. I was 135 pounds—normal for post-pregnancy. She took Christine from my arms and gave her to her husband Shane to mind while she herself started to clean. By the way, I am a perfectionist by nature, OCD in fact, and the place was already clean, believe me—another thing I inherited from my mother. I thought, *Will things ever change here?*

The one really good thing she did for me that really helped me feel better (as opposed to worse) was run a bath for me. I soaked in it for an hour. I was dying to go for a walk but didn't say in case that was seen as one of my tricks to "try to lose weight." She left a few hours later having bought me a baby changer, as obviously it was what I needed. I thanked her profusely, because of all the people that were a part of my life at the time, I saw that she was generous in monetary terms, and I appreciated her effort in this regard.

A few days later, Eoin suggested that I head home for a few days for a rest. We were arguing. I felt that he was not really here for me, and I see clearly now that he wasn't, but I was so depressed that all I could see was "my depression" and not the reality that had become my life—a life surrounded by addictive people.

So I went home to my sister Liz. Again she took over completely. I remember her putting Christine sleeping beside the kettle and hoover and anything that made noise. She smoked all around her (that bit really annoyed me) and basically took over as mother to Christine. She knew that I was incapable, and I knew that she knew. For Liz, I think she loved that she had at last found something I wasn't good at. I sensed that the controlling side of her relished this.

From there on in and especially in times of deep need, Liz took Christine from me. I remember once when Christine was about six months old; I arrived at Liz's for a night's break from Kilkenny. I left Christine sleeping, and as I was going out the door for a well-deserved walk I said to Liz (probably my third time to mention it, as it was important to me), "Please don't feed her chocolate—not yet. Later on she will have it, but just not yet. She is too young, at just less than six months. I want her to have only the best." Liz nodded at me, rolled her eyes to heaven to anyone else observing, and told me to go, be a good girl, and get some fresh air.

I arrived back an hour later to see Christine sitting beside the kettle as per usual in her high chair that Liz has picked out and bought eating a big chocolate biscuit. Liz came over to me grinning. She chuckled, "And that's her second one." It was by then beginning to dawn on me that while I was allowing Liz to take over from me as mother, she would. I knew deep down that I didn't have the strength to address this area of my life at this time—I was simply too exhausted working and paying the bills—and as long as Christine was happy, that was all that counted for the time.

From that time I began to escape into every self-help book imaginable. It was the summer of 2004, and thankfully there were a lot of self-help books to choose from. Susan Jeffers stands out in memory, *Feel the Fear and Do It Anyway*, but there were zillions of them. I drank them in. I ate them. My sisters told me that they were worried about my weight. They told me to eat more. Nobody worried about me, the inside me.

Shortly after Christine was born, Eoin asked me for more money. He asked for another ten thousand. He said he knew the game, the trading game, the day-trading game. He could do it he just needed a little cash, a starting point from which to flourish. He was still not working. He decided that this was what he was going to do. I gave him the money. I had it after all. The economy was going strong again in Ireland. I had just had the best year yet from a career perspective, and after all we were engaged. If we were ever to get married, then he simply had to make money.

I never saw the money again. I kept on reading, reading, and reading. I began to feel the pressure of the relationship on me. I began to get upset often. I began to resent Eoin for not having a job and for not having money of his own. I wanted to stay at home with Christine. I was on maternity leave and luckily with full pay, but I was very conscious that time was running out for me—I only had another few months before that time was up. Then I would have to go back. I wanted another child. Christine was so beautiful. But this—another child—was not meant to be. Instead it was time for me to confront my greatest fear—and that was that Eoin and I were possibly not meant to be.

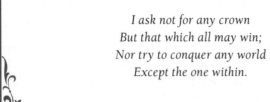

I ask not for any crown
But that which all may win;
Nor try to conquer any world
Except the one within.

Louisa May Alcott

CHAPTER 11

Wedding Bells, 2005

*E*oin had a great idea. He told me so. He had been thinking of it for some time, he said. He just wanted to be sure before he discussed it with me. He wanted to be sure it was the real thing, and it was. He explained how his friend Frank, who worked as a stockbroker, had an initial public offering first (sale of stock by a company to the public) that might make us a quick buck or two, and just before our wedding too. If we were lucky, he said we could get in and out on the same day, on the same day the stock first traded, and make a profit of twenty thousand.

This was a conservative figure he estimated because of the stock itself; it was as of yet a private American multinational in the biotechnology sector. It was a dead cert—it couldn't go wrong. And if the company in question didn't trade publicly or IPO as expected for whatever reason the money would be returned to our account and I could just take it all back to my own bank. I told Eoin that it was too much of a risk.

He persisted. Years later he admitted that he bullied me into it. It was easy to. All I wanted was for him to be happy. If he was happy, then we could get married and then I could finally be happy too. It was very simple really. I finally relented some two months later after countless long walks and lots of discussion. He told me that to get in like this, under the heading of "institution" stock, would mean that we would have to go in big. We would have to go in to the tune of seventy-five thousand. I was taken aback. I told him that I didn't have that kind of cash. He said not to worry, that his friend Alan could look after everything for us. He could remortgage my apartment, just for us, just this once. Eoin seem to have it all well thought through. I decided to trust him one more time.

Alan got us part thereof the money. I remortgaged my apartment with his help and got an additional sixty thousand in cash. I was still short twenty thousand by the time I paid Alan and legal fees. This was a setback. Eoin went back to the drawing board. I could see this was in the forefront of his mind. He wasn't going to be happy until this was sorted out. Out of pure desperation and after many countless more walks, he finally suggested that I go to the credit union for the rest of the funds. He knew that they had dealt with me in the recent past and had liked my credentials. I had always paid back every penny, and always on time.

So I did what he suggested. I went to the credit union in my local hometown where they knew me well. I got the money three days after my application; I got the extra twenty thousand and handed all seventy-five thousand of it over to Eoin. I trusted him; he knew what he was doing, and I knew that either way whatever happened I had been assured by him that I was going to get my seventy-five thousand back. He said that he was doing this for us and that it was all going to be an easy ride. We were lucky, he said, that we happened to be in the right place at the right time. This was going to work. I was convinced.

Prior to this Eoin and I had set a date for our wedding of September 9. It was to be on a Friday. We had it planned to take place in a newly renovated barn house outside Dungarvan, close to Waterford. Three weeks before our wedding was due to take place, Eoin broke down crying in our apartment. Our wedding invitations had been replied to; all was set. He had somehow always seemed strong and knowing to this point.

Eoin continued to cry. I tried to get him to look at me. He wouldn't. He was standing in front of our dishwasher leaning over himself, in our little kitchen. His head was down, his hands were over his eyes, and he was saying, "I can't, I can't," over and over again. Instantly it felt like it was déjà vu for me. I had done this when I was fifteen, in front of Liz. It must be really bad. Something really bad must have happened to him too.

"It's okay, Eoin. You can tell me," I whispered. "It's okay. Whatever it is it will be okay." Those same words that Liz had uttered to me so many years before. I was regurgitating what small snippets I have picked up along the way. I hoped it would work, and it did.

He looked up with a wild expression in his eyes like he was petrified. "I'm too embarrassed," he said, continuing, "too embarrassed to talk about it."

"Well, don't be, Eoin," I replied. "It's me."

By that point we had been living together on and off for five years. Surely there was nothing in the whole world that he couldn't tell me. Hadn't I told him every last detail of my childhood, at least that which I remembered at the time? He took a big gulped and blurted out, "It's the seventy-five thousand," he said. "It's gone. It's all gone." He looked down now again, afraid to look me in the eyes.

I thought I was going to faint. I reeled as the words slowly soaked in. My stomach did its usual flip; by then I was beginning to know when it was due to. All I could think of was what I had done. I had remortgaged my apartment and got a supplementary loan of twenty thousand in my name for this investment of ours. I hadn't planned in a million years on having to pay it back like this. Didn't he tell me that either way the money would come back to me? I hadn't planned for this at all.

Before I had time to go any further in our conversation, the phone rang. It was Eoin's mother. I crumbled. I was in such shock that I had to sit down, which I did before I picked up the phone. I was weak with worry. I tried to talk and found I couldn't.

~ 100 ~

"Hello. Hello. Hello," she repeated. I could tell that she was worried.

After a brief pause, I collected myself and responded, "It's me, Tara." But now I cut her off before she asked for Eoin as normally was the case, "I have just found out, Tara, that Eoin has lost all our money. I gave him seventy-five thousand, and he lost it."

There was silence for a few seconds before she reacted in horror. "Oh my God," she continued. "I have been so worried about him recently, Jean, so worried. I have been worried he would commit suicide. It's been that bad. We have been getting lots of post here on his behalf, from lots of different banks. I knew there was something wrong."

She paused again before confirming, "I'm so glad it's out now, Jean. I'm so glad he has come clean. Thank God we now know what's wrong. At least now we can deal with it." She paused. I was now in even more shock. *Is there anything I know about Eoin?* I thought to myself. "Lots of different banks?" I repeated slowly, my head going ninety in the background. What did this mean? I thought I had paid off all his old loans when I sold my house in Waterford. I thought all his old loans were gone.

"Yes," she continued, delighted to have gotten this off her chest. "We have been getting phone call too."

"Why didn't you tell me, Tara?" I asked meekly.

"We didn't know what to do. We decided it was best to wait and see. Eoin is his own man, you know. I mean it's been awful, just simply awful, Jean. But thank God we now know," she replied.

She concluded her part of conversation with "At my age I have very little to look forward to, and the very things that are important to me, the very things that are Shauna, Eoin, Sean, and Christine, well, simply put, I would do anything to protect them." She finished with "He is a good man, Jean, a good man."

I said little by way of reply. I ended the call as quickly as I could. She knew now that Eoin would call her to talk everything over when he was ready. She was relieved; I could tell. She couldn't wait to talk to Eoin separately later on in the evening. At least now she could do something to help him, to save him.

To me, this information was new and devastating—the old loans of Eoin's reappearing—and was one thing to think through. But by no means was it the worst thing that I had heard on that call. I thought maybe I had heard things so I repeated the sentence over and over in my mind. I think I may even have repeated it for years after just to be sure I hadn't misheard: "Shauna, Eoin, Sean, and Christine, well, simply put, I would do anything to protect them." I think I repeated it that day until I felt sick.

I didn't bother telling poor Eoin I felt sick. Poor Eoin—that was the message—poor Eoin, not poor Jean. There wasn't even a hint of that. I didn't feature in the whole conversation. I was irrelevant. He needed all the help he could get. *I must be a bad influence*, I thought.

We both needed help, so we each went home. We went our separate ways. We were both looking for support and comfort. I went home to my sister Angela's. I didn't go to my parents. I wished in hindsight that I had remained in Kilkenny, but I was still clinging to the hope that my family cared. Eoin went home to his worried mum and dad. I just went home because I simply had nowhere else to go.

I was visibly upset. I told Angela why I was upset on the way. I rang her to see if I could stay with her. She knew that I needed to talk. When I arrived, she was having dinner. I joined her. After dinner she was exhausted, too tired to talk, she said. She told me to sleep, that she couldn't take it all in; she promised that she would talk to me again in the morning.

She never did, and neither did I. She made me coffee, cooked me breakfast, chatted aimlessly. She never brought it up again. This was Angela. She avoided everything and anything linked to trauma like the plague, so I too was to be avoided like the plague. She did everything that day to distract herself. She even went shopping and bought me a new top in town, a token gesture. She was worried that I could see what she was really thinking. She was worried that I would ask her for money, and she was probably right to be. It was a money issue, and a serious one too.

I rang Eoin the next morning. I was fuming mad at him, but I needed him. I didn't have anyone else to talk to. I told him that

I needed him to come up to me; that we needed to talk; that I had no one to talk to. He was slow to, but he agreed. He didn't like my family, and my family didn't like him. This didn't surprise me; both had drawbacks, just like I did. Eoin's parents were great support, just what he needed, he said. I didn't feel the same way. I felt suicidal.

He arrived the following day around lunchtime. I was relieved. I had someone to talk to. We went for a long walk. We chatted for a time, and he seemed relaxed. I wasn't relaxed. I was a nervous wreck. He blamed my family for that. It was always my family's fault. They were never there for me. We needed to decide about our wedding, he said. His parents thought it was a bad idea to get married under the circumstances. He agreed, he said. It was for the best. I didn't think so. He was so calm and cool about it, like he was back in control, like we were all back to normal now. But this wasn't normal to me. This wedding, my wedding day, was the only thing in the world I had to look forward to, and now it wasn't even going to happen? *What about Christine?* I thought; this was for her too.

Eoin's father also told him that I needed to be strong in order for us to pull through this. Eoin said that he agreed with his dad.

I was confused, "Why do I need to be strong?"

He replied calmly, "If we are to get through it, if we are to survive this blip in our relationship."

I replied, lost in thought, "But I'm devastated."

Eoin looked at me with exasperation, "I'm devastated too, you know, Jean. This is devastating for me too. I had been looking forward to this too."

Didn't I understand that? Couldn't I see that? No, I couldn't. I couldn't at the time. I was in too much pain myself to see anyone else's.

We tried to talk to Angela again, the both of us. I don't know why; I think I was looking for somebody to tell me that this was all a very bad dream. No one ever did, though. This was my reality, and it was getting worse by the second. I wasn't sure if I could cope anymore. My outside persona of "normality" was beginning to break down, and if I let her go, I wasn't sure I would recover.

We finally cornered Angela the night before I went back to Kilkenny where I was due to return to work. Angela couldn't take it all in, she said. She was in shock, but she agreed that we shouldn't get married. She explained that she was in shock at the level of the loss to me. She observed that it was me who was carrying the can. She made a reference to Eoin being some kind of reckless maverick who had just gambled the money all away. Eoin later said he was never so insulted, to have been "dragged through the sewer" by Angela that day. He was never to forgive me for it.

I recall talking only one more time after that day to Eoin's mother and not again for a very long time. She told me to call her anytime, that she was there for me. In between I had relayed to Eoin what she had said. I never called. I didn't like her. I felt that she had turned Eoin into a mammy's boy. In fact I hated her. She was someone to take my pain out on. She was someone to deflect my anger on to. Why didn't she love me like she loved Eoin? Why didn't anyone love me?

Later Eoin reluctantly admitted to having gambled all of our money away. The money, seventy-five thousand, had returned into our Datek account (an account specifically for the direct buying and selling of shares) and not into my account, as the initial public offering never went ahead. Eoin said he got excited. He was convinced that he knew what he was doing. He felt comfortable "day trading," which you can only do with a Datek account, but he made a mistake. He had put a stop—set a price on which a stock automatically sells—one evening just before we headed out for a walk. He had done so incorrectly—it was much lower than what he had just bought it at—and by the time we came back in for our walk we had lost everything, all in the one day.

He thought if he could just make it big that would solve everything. It would solve all my financial insecurities, and it was solve all his problems. He knew that I wanted another child. He knew that I wanted to be at home. He knew that I craved security. He had wanted to give me that. Just as important to him was the fact that he wanted out of his line of work too. He was no longer interested in remaining in manufacturing. He wanted out. He lost everything too.

I simply died inside. I just didn't bother telling anyone. Nobody was listening anyhow. Eoin's parents were worried. I was jealous of that, how they worried about him. Mine weren't even worth talking to; and my poor sister Angela was exhausted inside too. I see that now.

*   *   *

Eoin and I returned separately to my apartment in Kilkenny, and I duly called work and all my family and friends and contacts and canceled our wedding. Eoin rang his mum and dad, who in turn called everyone invited on his side of the family to let them know that the wedding was canceled. My boss was very sympathetic. I said that my mother had broken her right arm from a serious fall; she actually had, and in the fall she had suffered a stroke. I told my boss that my mother would have been unable to attend the wedding at this time and so it was best we canceled for the time being until she was fully recovered. My mum had been drinking, secretly of course, at the time when this happened. She was crossing a road and fell down on her arm, broke it, and suffered a series of mini strokes. My boss listened and understood. She told me to take the week off. She told me to take as long as I needed.

I was in a haze. I had no one to turn to. I only had Eoin. So I did just that. I took a week off. Eoin and I went on our honeymoon as per normal. Nobody from home rang me. No one followed up. Nobody thought to say anything to me. Nobody knew what to do. Everything went back to normal. I simply picked up where we had left off; I continued to pay for everything, and I continued to talk to Eoin like we had a future. He acted as if we could salvage this.

I returned a week later and went to work. For a while I performed just like I had been taught to. I pretended to function like normal, as usual. I was consistent like that; no matter what, I performed as was expected of me. I was mature. There was no time for dramatics here; it was simply time to move on. No one said stop. No one was overly concerned. All thought it was a blip and that life would be back to normal in no time.

I don't know when along the line I came to the understanding or thought that my family was damaged. Like I said, over the years I read lots and lots of self-help books. I think subconsciously that I knew something was wrong, that this wasn't normal. I initially reached out to see what was wrong with me only to come to some sort of conclusion along the way that the rest of my family was not coping either; that they were damaged too; that they were surviving yes but not coping.

I realized that we were all damaged, just in different ways. We were a family full of damaged, uncaring individuals, lost souls. We had learned it from my parents. They hadn't cared for us, truly cared for us, and the unfortunate leaders of our family, whichever ones they were at the time, Angela first and then Liz, stuck to this very same mantle; it just manifested itself in different forms.

I also realized that nobody in our family listened either, just like our parents. We didn't listen to ourselves. We didn't listen to others. We couldn't hear. We were exhausted. We were weak just like our parents. We were surviving as best as we could. We lost ourselves in money matters, just like our parents did, and we forgot to care. We threw money at the problem. Small amounts were doled out every now and then, and they were small compared with the level of wealth attained at the time.

For those unfortunate enough not to have money, we had to resort to begging for monetary help, just like our parents let us grovel for every single last penny. We weren't really worthy of being saved, but grudgingly they did it anyway. If for no other reason it was so that the neighbors might not find out about this latest tragedy or mishap. It was important to keep everything under the radar. Let us look like we are a happy family; let's pretend; let's just keep on pretending. And so we did—well, most of us did.

It was at this point—a very humbling experience—that I decided that I was going to continue to care. They didn't. My mum and dad didn't, but I did. Angela and Liz didn't really care anymore—well, maybe occasionally Liz still did. But there it was—such a simple statement but decisively the opposite of anything I had ever known and that was—I was going to continue to care. The piece that I had gotten wrong up until then was that I had cared about other people to the detriment of myself. Maybe that was due to the fact that no one else did. Maybe I didn't think I deserved to be cared for. Nobody had really cared, not really—well, not much anyhow. They didn't need to.

To the outside world I was strong and responsible. I was a formable survivor, not like my brother Tom. I had done well for myself. I had built a web of lies around me; I even lied to myself. I pretended that all was well. I pretended that I was living, not merely surviving, not merely existing. No one saw the real me. I didn't show it to them. But somewhere deep inside I decided that I was going to care about me and my life and what was happening to it.

Deep down I was determined not to turn into Angela, in particular the person she had become. I didn't like what I saw in her. She had become helpless and uncaring like my mother. In my eyes she had turned into my mother. I was determined that I wasn't. That route wasn't for me. I was simply going to keep right on caring, even if it killed me. That was better than slowly turning into my poor helpless pitiful mother. Anything was better than that. I was angry, but care I still did. I had made a decision, and like clockwork I was sticking to it.

Eoin and I split up within a year of his losing the money. He tried his best to recover what we had, but something inside me wouldn't let him back in. A wall appeared between us, and I knew that I couldn't bring it back down. Instead I continued to read, and I started to pray. As I hadn't yet forgiven the church for their imposing ways, ways that impacted the women of Ireland beyond recognition, I chose instead to pray alone. I did, though, reach out for help by going to counseling. I went for years. I decided that it was time to get to know the real me. It wasn't easy. I had so many layers of denial wrapped around me that I wasn't sure who I was. I guess

I was desperately trying to extract myself from the mistakes of my past. It was to be a long road.

I decided to tell my counselor the truth as I saw it. I told her that I knew that I was at a point now in my life where both Angela and Liz had been previously. I also told her of the rest of my family—of my eldest brother Tom, who was by now a heroin addict, and that there was no getting him back. The rest of the family, whom I referred to as followers, remained in hiding, quietly suffering in silence. They had their routine sure, but it was one that avoided change at any cost. They were sticking staunchly to it. They couldn't handle change. They had looked at what change went on throughout Angela's and Liz's lives and said to themselves, *I'm not taking any risks here; this is what risk lead to. It always leads to a bad outcome.* And now I was one of them too. I was a leader who had taken risks and failed. I just further confirmed this to them, and they concluded, "This is not what we are supposed to do in life. Our leaders are wrong."

In my counselor I found a true friend, though I'm not sure I always viewed her that way at the time. She always gave me a big hug at the end of each session, confirming to me how well I was doing. Initially when I explained that I was sexually abused, she said in a lovely long Scottish drawl, "We will come back to that later, Jean. We will come back to that. For the moment, we will concentrate on your present and how we are going to get you out of this." I laugh thinking of her, as at times she took me by surprise. Her directness was not always welcomed, but the sentiment was always factual and truthful.

One day after many months of counseling me, she turned to me and pointedly said, "Jean, you need to view yourself as an orphan. You need to understand that you do not have a family. Do you hear me? I know that sounds harsh, but it's true. It is the only way you will get yourself out of this current mess. You need to rely on you and no one else. Choose your friends wisely, and keep them close. Your family cannot be here for you for this. They are simply not able."

For a time I became a tired and worn-out single working mum. I paid back two large loans inside a year. I focused on little else. I was dead inside and wasn't ready to live again, so I worked and worked, and in between I gave Christine what little love I had. She was my little bundle of joy and the only thing that got me out of bed in the morning. In her I saw hope—for the future.

I hired two ladies to help me with minding her. This was separate to her Montessori school, which she attended from morning till evening five days a week. I decided that if I couldn't give her the love she so clearly needed, then it was best to hire someone to help me with fulfilling her needs. It was the best thing to do at the time. It was all I could do at the time.

Death makes angels of us all
And gives us wings
Where we had shoulders
Smooth as raven's
Claws.
Jim Morrison, The American Prayer

CHAPTER 12

Dad's Passing, 2007

here were many events that took place leading up to my dad's death that had a lasting impact on me at the time. It was like they were little pieces of the jigsaw puzzle finally beginning to fall into place. It helped me to understand a lot about my family, our culture, and of the impact of alcoholism on us all.

The first was around the time Dad was diagnosed with cancer. My sister Liz had diligently brought him in for a third checkup in so many months. Every test showed up negative. Given his drinking habit, a lot of the tests were around his heart. It was only by chance on the day when he was ready to leave hospital once again with the all clear that he coughed and in doing so coughed up blood in front of the nurse on duty. With that she held off discharging him and the doctors took a second look, focusing only on his throat.

It turned out to be cancer of the throat. It was all over, including in his lymph nodes and also partly in his lungs. It had gone "secondary" as soon as the word lymph had been used. From that day in February 2006 it was all downhill for Dad.

Dad wasn't able to endure chemotherapy treatment, so that got pushed to the side almost immediately. His system was too weak. So radium treatment was considered as his best option. We were told that there was a 50/50 chance of a positive result with this, and unfortunately Dad turned out to be in the wrong 50 percent category. I was with Mum when the doctors told her the news, having taken a few days off from work to be with them both.

It wasn't a surprise. We had been waiting all our lives for this moment. We had talked about it often. "It's only a matter of time," one would say, and the other would always agree, "Yes it is." It was inevitable. There was no way back for Dad. In our heart of hearts we knew that; we knew he had gone too far—to the point of no return. And so when it happened—when the word was out and it was clear there was no going back—there wasn't any big reaction. There was nothing—just maybe a quiet despairing acceptance. This wasn't just a sad ending; this was a sad and unnecessary one.

That night I cried myself to sleep like I had never done before; not even the partner losses of Rob and Eoin from my life could touch on the pain I felt on that night. It was like that of a lone wolf, heart piercing and bewildered. I woke up with swollen eyes. Mum said nothing, and I said nothing. I couldn't. I didn't fully understand at the time why I cried like that.

It's only now as I look back that I realize that mourning the loss of my dad, a dad I never had, allowed me to also mourn the loss of so many other areas of my life. I had a reason to mourn—I had a cover, a front. Up to this point, I had always been on the run … literally. I had focused solely on the future and nothing else. I hadn't allowed myself any time to mourn the loss of any part of my past, but on that night for many reasons—the trigger being my dad—it all came roaring out of me. It felt good to finally let it all out; it was such a relief!

I couldn't see the next day. I had arranged the day before to meet Rob, having not seen him for six years, and here I was not looking my best to say the least. Rob was as always lovely and considerate of both my dad and me. He had come to visit my dad on my relaying the news of his cancer to him. After Rob had left, my dad, who normally was never one to make comment on someone's looks turned, and said, "My God, I had forgotten how good-looking he is!" He was right.

Rob had been a gorgeous boyfriend in every way except we had ended up being incompatible. It had been as simple as that, and at last I was beginning to find a place of peace within me for that choice. I was beginning to accept me as I was, for the deeply driven person that I was. I was always striving for something more suitable for me, and at this point in my life I was still on my quest.

*   *   *

Leading into Christmas, my sister Maria returned home from Canada to visit Dad. By now Mum and Dad had permanently moved in with Liz. As Maria was only ever home for a short period at a time, I made the effort to drive home to visit her. Maria was staying in my sister Liz's house minding Dad for the weekend. This was to give my sister Liz and her husband a break away, one that they very much deserved.

A tube had by now been attached externally to my Dad's stomach as the only means of giving him basic nutrition; his throat could no longer function. But this didn't stop him from trying to put alcohol into his mouth when it literally had nowhere to go. There was no real change here—not even in the face of death.

Physically Dad was beginning to look like a shell of his former self. Maria was very sentimental about this, and even though Dad had not been there for her much in the later years, she still saw it as appropriate to care for him in his darkest hours. I didn't feel the same way. I never knew my dad. I remembered that he was kindhearted and funny, but he had never been there for me physically or emotionally. He had never made the effort to visit me in any one of my hard-earned homes except to my daughter's christening, and then it was only for a few miserable hours. So to me I was not outwardly concerned that he was dying. In fact I was kind of happy for him and us all to be honest. I thought it might give Mum back the life she truly deserved, along with Liz and her family.

Throughout Dad's year-long illness Liz had made a point of caring for him around the clock, to the detriment of her sleep, my sister Joan's sleep, and my mum's sleep (I'm sure Mum didn't really mind, as this was where she had always wanted to be). Liz had six children and heavy work commitments, and Joan too worked full-time self-employed and had her own children to look after.

Out of a sense of allegiance, Joan spend one night a week fully awake with Dad as a way of helping Liz keep this commitment to a man who had never once kept a commitment (of being a father) to her. I found this fascinating. I knew that my dad was a good man underneath and like I said previously possessed a wicked sense of humor, but I thought Liz took on a very onerous burden both personally and for the extended family.

This was a real eye opener for me, one that made me think of my own death. I have since visualized myself peaceful in my rocking chair in my garden basking in the sun—gracefully going to the next world in my sleep. I would like to go into my later years mentally and physically strong so that the image I have here is a real possibility. Of course I know that Christine would be happy to help me in small ways, but I would never want it to be in a way that would be detrimental to her own (and her own family's) health and well-being. To me what Liz did was extremely unhealthy, but then again that is what alcoholism does to you—it walks over (and back again) all boundaries. It has no respect for the person it consumes or for others entrapped in it. It is all consuming. This was one very valuable lesson I have since learned, that nothing in our external life should be this all consuming.

One particular time I had come to visit Maria to take her out for a walk and catch up. I entered Liz's house and continued through the myriad of corridors and hallways till I came to Dad's downstairs room. Maria was standing next to Dad's bed. She was fluttering around and making a fuss over him. She then asked him if he wanted the shutters left open or shut. I interjected and told her to leave them open. Through the window was the most spectacular view anyone could wish for. I told Dad so. He agreed. It was sunny out, and from his bed Dad could see a series of beautifully man-crafted slow descending mini waterfalls leading on to a stunning display of green shrubbery and apple trees. My sister's mansion was magnificent, and this part of the garden showed its magnificence to perfection. I told Dad he was so lucky to have this room in his illness. He acknowledged, weakly nodding in reply. Liz had his room done up like a hospital ward, just even more pristine and opulent, a thing that only Liz could do with such style.

I told him that I had come to bring Maria for a walk—that she needed a break. I knew that he was most likely wishing he could come too, but he was just too ill to. By now he was barely able to get into his wheelchair, and after any more than twenty minutes in it he got mildly flustered by way of acknowledging his need to get back into his bed to rest.

Maria said her good-byes, and off we went down the back lane, over a gate, out around a small bridge, and up a small winding laneway. We began chatting about all that was happening around us. How Dad was dying, how sad it was, how Liz was taking such good care of him, and how we all were lucky to have this time with him.

Maria started to tell me this story of when she finally realized Liz had made it, in monetary terms. What other terms were there? It's a family trait. For her it was when she happened to come upon Liz's walk-in wardrobe and saw all the different types of boots Liz had. She had never seen such choice and color, and she talked of this in detail. I laughed like never before. I couldn't help but make a joke of what she said.

Maria looked at me as if I were mad but later joined in the fun. "So, Maria, the mile-long tar macadam well-lit driveway—and I mean well lit—with endless well-tended gardens, a twenty thousand square foot beautifully adorned house and suitable surrounding walls along with acres of stables, a helicopter pad, and a gazillion shiny cars out front did nothing for you then?" I smugly said, finishing with, "It was the boots that gave it all away. Well, Maria, you are a classic!" I thought her so innocent and charming.

At that moment my mobile rang. I answered it; it was Liz. We had been gone about twenty minutes or so. I could barely take in all that was being said as Liz was raving on the phone. She was delirious with anger. She was telling me that she couldn't believe that she was gone only a short time and already she had got a phone call from her daughter to say that our mother was on the floor drunk at home. Obviously we were not to be trusted having acted so irresponsibly as to have gone for a walk without thinking of our mother's every detrimental move, not to mention leaving Dad alone! Heaven forbid!

We quickly turned back to rescue Liz's daughter from our mother's wayward way. It was the very least we could do for a sister who had spent her every living hour keeping Dad happy in his final hours alongside his darling wife. That was the sentiment, and by God, did we get it! We arrived back—running—into the fold like little bad schoolgirls who had left their station without permission from the head nun. Liz's daughter stood at the doorway with a look of disgust. I thought after it was no wonder my sister never asked me to mind Dad; sure I was obviously totally irresponsible.

I was by now a manager with many direct reports and the primary guardian and provider to my daughter. I had also kept myself together while carrying a lot of debt—debt that I knew I would carry for the rest of my days. That was just life. I had made the mistake of letting it happen through my lack of awareness, but once I became aware, my personal relationships began changing for the better. To my mind what Liz was suggesting wasn't in my view any way appropriate or in proportion. Was it my job to control everyone's every move? Was that healthy? After that day, I harbored a little resentment toward my sister; I think a sense of realism was finally setting in.

Later that evening I was chatting to Dad, and out of nowhere I turned and said, "Dad did you ever think to say sorry to Mum?"

He immediately turned toward me, startled. He said the first thing that came into his head, "No, why?" He was amazed as to why he would need to say sorry, I could tell.

I paused thoughtfully and then calmly replied, "Well, you know there were many nights where Mum waited patiently for you to come home from the pub and you'd never come home when she was expecting you. You would arrive back very late, and most of the time you were very drunk and we would have to carry you in the door. Do you remember any of those nights?"

He was instant in his reply. There was no argument or defensiveness in his reply, "No, I don't remember that at all." He was pensive then, trying to remember, I guess.

I continued, "Well, it was tough on her, really tough, and maybe you should say something to her about it. Maybe you could try to say sorry."

He thanked me profusely and said adamantly, "Yes I will. I will do that."

I left the following morning. On the drive back I was struck with how my dad had given no consideration whatsoever to his self-destructive past. I realized then from his reaction, as it was so genuine, that he most likely had not even remembered any or most of it. It was all a blank to him, as it was most likely to my mother in her later years. Now how sad is that?

To think that you would live your life like my mother did in the early years waiting for the man of her dreams to come home and he simply doesn't even remember to and not only that but he doesn't even remember enough to someday go toward repairing a relationship with this lovely woman he claims to love so adamantly. It all seems a little too sad for words, in my opinion. I have since concluded that it couldn't be worth it—this kind of love is not worth it. It makes me think that you have to live every second being fully aware and happy of all the good around you—don't take the good for granted, but rather choose to enjoy it like it's your last moment on earth, because before you know it is.

* * *

At this time I was in a new relationship and it was arriving at a stage where James was due to be introduced to my family, so I invited him up to meet with all in our home town. We had only been dating a few months, but everyone was curious to meet with him. It was my first relationship after Eoin; everyone was happy I had at last moved on.

Unfortunately he was never to make a return visit, as our relationship came to a natural end within the year. Our personalities were very different. Again, like Rob, he was too laid back to be a fit with me, and I in turn was too controlling of him. I always gave off that sense that I knew where I was going, even if I didn't always know. Thankfully James had the courage to end our relationship—citing our differencing personalities as the reason—a gesture I am now very grateful to him for.

We had just arrived at my sister Liz's home. I remember leaving James behind me to going through the kitchen/living room area to get some tissue for Christine. It was then that I saw Dad at the back of the room in his wheelchair. It was almost like he was waiting for me, and I sensed that he wanted to say something quickly to me before he got too tired to. Mum was ever present standing close by. At last she had him where she had always wanted and needed him—by her side. It was genuinely a lovely sight to see. She looked content.

Dad looked up into my eyes just before his wheelchair started to move. He stared directly at me and said with a quick burst of energy, "You'll be okay. You'll be fine. I don't need to worry about you."

I said nothing. It was a curious thing to say, I thought. I certainly didn't feel that way at the time. I turned and nodded gently for James to come over and join me while I introduced him to my mum and dad. Everyone shook hands before Mum nodded that it was time for Dad to go. She wheeled him back to his bed to rest. This family gathering was to be the second-to-last time I was to see Dad before he passed away.

*   *   *

It had been a particularly hectic and successful time leading up to the usual Christmas holidays. So it was with this in mind as well as being the only singleton in the family that I planned Christmas in my sister Liz's house with her family and Mum and Dad. Liz was always very welcoming at this time of the year—she simply loved everything about Christmas—and it was with a light heart that I set off home that Christmas Eve thinking of all the last-minute things I had to do before the big day arrived.

I had barely arrived inside the door of the house when Dad, in his wheelchair at the end of the kitchen table, turned to me as if he again had been waiting for me. Again I sensed that he was tired and flustered, so I knew to go over to him and save him from wasting any little energy he had left. This time his question was about him, not me.

He was serious and agitated as he blurted out, "How long does it take to die?"

For some reason I didn't even think to wait to respond. I just simply leaned down before him and replied as gently as I could, "I guess, Dad, when you decide to die then it is time to die."

He thought about what I said and nodded, "Yes," he said. "You're right. When you decide then it's time to go." He seemed happy with my response. I was a practical person like him. I had just given it to him straight. It was the way he had wanted to hear it.

My Dad died in late January, having struggled all the way through Christmas. I was the last person to arrive at his bedside, as it had taken me two hours to travel home. He had just passed away by the time I reached him, so all I could do was put my hand on his forehead, kiss him, and say, "It's okay to go, Dad; it's okay to go."

We called Maria in Canada to let her know that Dad had passed away. Shortly after this Maria rang my sister Angela to seek her advice about coming home. Really what Maria was saying was, "I have just paid to come home and see Dad, and I'm not sure I can afford to come back again." Maria was always on a tight budget, and she had worked hard to get to see Dad a few times before he passed away. Her latest visit came to an end just a week before he passed away. Angela's response was along the lines of "Maria, don't worry about coming home; you were only just here."

Later that evening Maria rang me and told me in passing of her conversation with Angela. Luckily I picked up on Maria's upset. I told her not to worry; that if we had to wait weeks we would; and that it was more important we were all together for Dad's funeral than anything else. After the call I talked to Liz. She too saw the need to bring Maria home, and she called Maria back to let her know she would pay for her flight.

Liz and I laughed at Angela and her lack of heart at emotional times such as these. It didn't matter what you did, said, or felt—she just didn't get it; sometimes she could say nice words, but even then her whole body and subsequent reactions showed that she just didn't mean it.

We waited three days for Maria to come home from Canada. Everything went in to automatic drive from the word go. Liz's house was constantly full of people, and everyone was drinking and telling stories of my dad of old—the ones about how successful he was, how he loved to attend local football and hurling matches, and how he enjoyed being out and about meeting and talking with everyone who came across his path. There was no doubt that he had been a lively character.

Of course, no one dared talk of his drinking habit. That was to be forgotten—only the good remained. Liz and Shane took over completely with regard to the funeral arrangements. They did so in a style like I had never seen before. Their house was an open house to all who wanted to visit Dad and say their last good-byes—for three whole days and nights, tens and tens of bottles of spirits later.

Liz and Shane arranged for the immediate family, all thirty-something of us, to be escorted by black limousine-style Mercedes. There were almost half a dozen cars in all. As we drove through our small town toward the graveside Liz turned to Mum and said, "Dad would love this, Mum, wouldn't he?" She was referring to the commotion we were causing in the town with what can only be described as a "celebrity style" funeral in action.

Mum nodded happily, "Yes he would."

He would in my ass, I thought. This wasn't Dad; this was Mum. Of the two, she loved to be the center of attraction. I thought it farcical, embarrassingly so. Who did we think we were? Important? Maybe we were more important than someone else? I thought we were born equal and die equal? Whatever happened to this concept? I said nothing, of course. I decided that it was best to stay quiet. I'm glad I did.

At the graveside, I took some time out to observe all that was happening around me. I gazed at all the black cars with blacked-out windows. I saw the crowds looking at us; I too looked at us all. As a family we looked very together. I took a closer look at Mum. She was beautiful in all her finery, her makeup and hair done to perfection, not a thing out of place, not a tear to be seen. I thought, *How fake we all look. There is nothing sincere in this.* Again I said nothing out loud.

Liz then turned and instructed one of the drivers to open the trunk of her car. Before I knew it there was a stack of white boxes filled with hundreds of single red roses on the ground before me. Liz nodded to me as if willing me to take one and put it on Dad's coffin before it was due to be covered up. I went red with embarrassment. I bent down, took one, and threw it lightly on to Dad's coffin. My family followed suit. There were so many flowers that Liz encouraged others outside the family to do the same. Some did; some didn't. I had to throw a few more in just to get through them.

I walked away thinking to myself, *If I die, then I must make sure to let my family know that I absolutely do not want to be buried this way. Let me die in an unmarked grave before I go this way, please God.* It was a day I was happy to forget for all the wrong reasons; this was beginning to be the story of my entire life.

The most memorable moment of my dad's funeral for me was when I got to talk to Rob. He came to pay his respects. I was delighted to see him and to see him so happy. I was quite emotional with him as I walked him to his car to say good-bye. Just before he opened his car door he turned to say, "I'm sorry, you know."

I queried, "Sorry for what?"

He looked me straight in the eye and said, "For not being there for you. I should have been. I wished I had, but I wasn't."

I thought him so kind to say those words. They took my breath away. Tears of relief welled up in my eyes. "Thank you," I uttered. "Thank you so much."

He hugged me. After that the conversation lightened up. I told him how delighted I was for him. I knew he was very happy in his marriage and with his newborn child. I told him I knew we were not meant to be but that I was grateful to have had him in my life. He talked about how he loved the house he had built (on the site we were supposed to build on together once upon a time) and how he was still into his cars and bikes. He talked of having bought a new motorbike and how he had just come back from a week in Italy with two of his male friends. He said, "It's the only way to go—to have a passion that's just yours. It's one way of ensuring you don't have an affair!" I laughed thinking of this afterward. He had obviously felt the same way as I had at the end of our relationship.

He was right, of course. I see that now. It was to be a little while before I truly understood this statement for what it was. I see now that it is staleness in a relationship that breeds depression. I had sucked the life out of all my past relationships. I had such a strong need to control everything that I didn't allow time for solutions to problems. I never allowed for space. My overpowering craving for company (due to a lack of it in my childhood) was to the detriment of all my relationships. I took passion out of the equation in favor of predictability.

*   *   *

A few months later, I went on holidays to Sardinia with a girlfriend of mine. It was a painful time for me. It was the first time since my dad's funeral that I allowed time for my feelings for him to come to the surface. I reflected on the sad end my dad had to his life; on the sad end we all had come to relative to him. It was hard not to blame it all on money. It was his failing. Money had gotten the better of him. It could have made him stronger, having given him all the time in the world to reflect and move on gratefully and gracefully, but instead it brought him down; it led him to an easy life of drink.

It was then that I also reflected on the ostentatious nature of Dad's funeral and the wealth he had amassed over his lifetime, and yet I was still struggling financially as I had been before his passing. My plight was never a consideration of Dad's or in his estate thereafter, and somehow that just didn't seem fair to me or to other members of my family.

In my opinion Dad had taken the wrong road. I knew that I too was continuing on the wrong road. I knew that I needed to change direction, but I had little guidance or the kind of leadership I was looking for within my vicinity. But inadvertently by even asking these questions, I was sending myself on a path of self-discovery and ultimately one of true happiness. It was to be a rocky road to start.

Just before Dad died I met a married man who was to become my best friend. It happened almost without my being aware at first. For me he was to become my guardian angel and one of the most beautiful people I have ever had the pleasure to meet. His name was Paul, and with his emotional support, I took the plunge and left my full-time pensionable job and took up flexible consultancy work. It was with his guidance I slowly started to live a freer life—one where predictability wasn't a sacrifice.

When one door closes another one always opens.

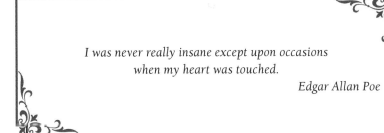

*I was never really insane except upon occasions
when my heart was touched.*

Edgar Allan Poe

CHAPTER 13

A Best Friend

September 2008

*P*aul and I were friends for a long time before any other thoughts surfaced in my mind. I had met him at a work seminar. A mutual friend had introduced us, and from the moment we met, we were the best of buddies. Paul was much older than me, eighteen years, and his initial focus was always on my potential. He saw it even when I didn't. He was so supportive of me in all ways that eventually, with his help, I left my permanent pensionable job to move into consultancy. He had lots of contacts and had no hesitation recommending me to those with whom he also worked.

In that time, we ended up going overseas and generally spending a lot of time together. In all these times, he was professional and respectful in his approach to me—others weren't always. As a result, I trusted him like no one else. He too felt the same way, as over time he talked a lot of his marriage and how he was struggling to make it work. He was at a point where he was trying to encourage his wife to go on a date night with him during the week, but no matter what he did, he felt that he couldn't get through to her. Obviously there was history between them I didn't know of, nor did I want to. The only thing that really mattered in the end was that he was moving closer to me while at the same time moving further and further away from his wife. It all happened with Paul and me being unaware. Now I would be so much more aware.

At the same time I was dating someone else, but it was obvious from the beginning that it wasn't going to work. I realize only now that I have lots of alpha female traits—to be in the driver seat and to relish work over staying at home. The person I was dating at this time felt threatened by this, and so understandably we parted. Of course I turned to my best friend for solace, and without warning we fell in love.

*   *   *

An incident stands out in my mind around the time I knew I had begun to have deeper feelings for Paul. It was the day after he had told me he loved me. He loved me and wanted to be with me. He had been in Dublin for the day on business and was calling me on his way home. He told me that he wanted to stop his car to tell me something, that it was important. He told me that he had just realized something and he wanted me to know. It was then that he told me that he loved me. I didn't say anything in reply; it was only later that I texted him to say I was worried.

The next day he came over for his usual cup of coffee and chat. It was early in the morning, before we had to part ways and go to work. He did that often, came over for morning coffee; this was our special time together. He later told that me he could see my loneliness, that he could see it through my strength, my exterior. He usually brought scones too from the local cottage shop. They went perfectly with my frothy coffee. I knew I made lovely coffee just the way he liked it.

"Well, tell me," he said. "Come sit beside me; you look upset. Tell me how I have upset you." I sat beside him; he put his arm gently around me, as if to protect me from the world. "If only they would leave us to it," he would say, just as his father had said to him. "If they left it to us, sure we'd solve all the problems of the world." It used to make me laugh, the way he would say it. I could be in the throes of giving out, procrastinating even, and he would say, "Ah, if only they could leave it to us, sure all would be fine."

I said, "I'm not sure what I want to say, Paul. I'm not sure how I feel."

He said, "Well, what is it you think you feel?"

I said, "I know I love you. I know I love everything about you, but it's just the age thing. I don't think I can deal with that. I think there is too much of an age gap between us. I think it's the eighteen years. I know that in every other way we connect, but I think the age gap is too much."

He said, "That's okay, you know."

I replied, "I have something else, Paul, that I need to tell you. It's about my childhood. I was abused, sexually abused, badly so. One of the abusers was Dad's foreman. He was old, very old. I think that may have something to do with it too. I'm not too sure."

He said, "That's okay too, you know. That's okay. I love you. I love you enough to accept what you are saying to me. I understand if you can't do this. I understand completely. We can and will go back to being the best of friends. That's okay too. Now come here and let me hug you as a friend. I will always be here for you as a friend. Don't ever forget that."

I cry just thinking of those words now. I cry for their beauty. I cry thinking how kind he was. How lovely he was. I cry with appreciation.

Shortly after that day, Paul and I became an item. He had listened. He had heard me, and I loved him all the more for it. This was the first time in my life when I felt loved and accepted for who I was. This was the first time in my life when someone had listened and acted, acted like they really cared. Here was someone willing to put me first.

Jean Berry

For a long time, we just kissed. There was good reason for this. Paul was still living a married life. He knew that I was more than unhappy about that; I had told him so from the beginning. He knew it, but he wasn't ready to make the break just yet; he had to think everything through, so we kissed, talked, kissed, and left it at that. It was coming close to Christmas, and I was feeling lonely. I think Paul could sense that. He could sense what a lonely time of the year it was for me. He knew that Christine was all of my responsibility. He knew that it wasn't fair. He had seen firsthand how Eoin would switch prearranged custodial arrangements with me at a moment's notice. He also observed how Eoin would financially support Christine and me while there was hope of a reunion; when there wasn't, something appropriately came up that caused him to discontinue.

Christine was the one to suffer most at this time. She became clingy for a time—looking for assurance that she was loved and wanted. It took all my energy at the time to hold down my job and keep a roof over our head, and trying to give extra attention to Christine on top of this was making my life impossibly hard. Paul knew this and sympathized. He would often just appear in the evening, inviting Christine out to feed the ducks. He knew that I needed rest. He always gave to me in bundles.

It was then when I decided—out of the blue—to take a risk with Paul. I arranged for him to come over and stay the night, no strings attached. All strings were attached, of course. I took the risk, I think, because I needed him. I needed to have some hope in all of the despair I always felt. When we finally slept together it was lovely—it was more than lovely. He was truly beautiful inside and out. He shined with enthusiasm; he shined with love. We were madly in love.

I went home for Christmas and said nothing. Paul was married—there was nothing to say. I knew that it was bad timing to bring it up with him. I knew that I had to leave it till after Christmas, so that's what I did. Shortly after, I asked to talk to him. He knew what it was about. He knew that he had to make a choice. He knew that it was going to be the most difficult decision of his life. He loved his family, including his wife. He just couldn't seem to get through to her. More recently, he had told her that he was unhappy. They had argued. She just argued back. No decisions were being made. I was getting frustrated, and so was Paul.

Around this time Paul and I had our one and only argument—he was a hard man to argue with. One day out of the blue I turned to him and said, "You know you have got the better deal here."

"How?" he replied curiously.

"Well, for example, you get to be seen out with a younger woman," but before I got to finish the sentence he turned to me and said with an underlying of controlled anger in his voice, "If you think for a second I am in this because you are younger than me, then you are very much mistaken. Do you really think I want to be seen out with a younger woman? You must be joking. It's the opposite of everything I stand for. The last thing I want is to be seen out and about with a younger woman or even be in a relationship with a much younger woman. I have fallen for you, the person you are inside, not for what you look like on the outside. Let's make that perfectly clear, and let's make it perfectly clear that I would much prefer to be with a woman my own age, but unfortunately that is not to be the case here."

I didn't argue with him again on this point. I knew I had been incorrect in my thinking and relayed this to him shortly thereafter.

Regardless, by March things were close to an end for Paul and me. I was running out of patience. I knew one thing for sure, that no matter how much Paul said he loved me, if he didn't move on, then he didn't love me enough. I knew that I had Christine to consider. I knew that she deserved to know the man in my life and have him in her life too. This was breaking point for us. I gave Paul space. I stopped making contact with him. I knew that I had to start the process of letting go. I was devastated.

But then, just as I had given up hope, Paul called. He said, "I need to see you. I have left. I have nowhere to go. Anne got up early this morning, came into my room, and told me to leave. So I did. I did what she said. I'm out, J, I'm out."

"Okay, come over," I replied calmly—I wasn't going to get my hopes up too quickly. He came over, and I made him coffee. We talked some more. He told me how he had to go into his children's room and tell them he was leaving. He was very upset. He had wanted to do it differently, but he knew that Anne was upset. He knew that she had every reason to be upset. He knew that he was destroying her world—a world she had tried hard to control. He didn't stay long.

I knew he needed space, so I let him go. He went to his friend Mannie's house and told him what happened. Mannie was shocked. This was his best friend. He and his wife had been best friends with Paul and his wife for many years. This was devastating for them too. Mannie knew I was the reason. He didn't want me to be the reason. I knew that he thought I was not good for Paul, that I was too young. I knew that he wanted Paul to give up his mad idea of his and just go back to Anne.

I felt like an outsider, but I had felt like that before, and so I guess while it bothered me, it didn't really bother me. All I cared about at that point in time was that Paul loved me enough to give up all that he had, his wife and family, to be with me. I somehow felt blessed even amid the devastation, and I knew that it was heartbreaking for Paul and for all of those around him.

Paul never went back home from that day forth. He moved into a house later that day outside Kilkenny. At this stage, Anne didn't know about me. In the weeks that followed, Paul, Christine, and I went everywhere together. We spent long evenings at Paul's barbecue out back chatting, dancing, and singing over a bottle of wine and steak while Christine chased wild rabbits that popped up every now and then. Paul also enjoyed a lovely relationship with my sister Angela in particular. In the early days, I had tried to introduce Angela to Paul, as I thought it might work in the long run. However, Paul could never take his eyes off me long enough to even see Angela. As it turned out Paul wasn't really Angela's type—which was good news—so a solid friendship followed.

*　*　*

Six weeks later, completely unexpectedly, Paul died. He died with me. He had a heart attack beside me, fell to the ground, and died. He died before his mother died. He died young, just like his dad. Paul had been the head of his family. He had taken on his father's role when he was dying, so I knew deep down that this was a significant death for all concerned.

I can remember when Paul died being very much in control (on the outside). I can remember calling his best friend, Mannie, first to let him know that Paul had had a heart attack, that I had called the ambulance, that they had come and taken him away, that it was not good. I knew that Paul was dead, but I didn't say it. I just let him know that it was not good. I then rang Paul's other friend next, Derek, and told him. I knew that he would know better what to do. I knew that he was good in crisis. I knew the behaviors. I had seen them before in my sister Liz.

Derek came and took all of Paul's belongings from my home. He hugged me and left. He didn't stay for tea. I circled my two-bedroom apartment a few times. I felt better for doing it, so I continued to do it. I rang my sister Liz to let her know. She sent her daughter, Beth, who was in college nearby, over to me. Beth made me tea; her mother had told her so. Liz rang me back a few times to plead with me to take brandy with it. I didn't. I couldn't. I was too upset.

Angela then rang me. She was on her way down to me. At this point it was 2:00 a.m. Paul had been dead three hours. I continued circling the kitchen. Beth just looked at me. She asked me to relax, to have another cup of tea. I said I was relaxed, just upset, and that this was the best I could do for the moment. I checked in on Christine a few times. She was fast asleep. I thanked God for that. I thanked God that she was still breathing, that at least he hadn't taken her away. I knew that would have been worse, to lose your child—that would be so much worse.

I continued circling the room, thinking and thinking. I don't think I said another word to Beth. I didn't want to. I thought that if I said anything, I would lose it. I would lose it and kill myself. I wanted to throw myself off a cliff. I wanted to die. I felt like it was the end of the world. It was the end of the world to me. *Where do I go now? What do I do now? How do I get through this? This unbearable pain, will it ever go away?* Just when I thought it might go away, it was back, a hundredfold. I couldn't bear it; I couldn't bear the pain of it. I thought I was going mad.

I lay down on my bed, the bed that Paul had just died in. I lay down on my side. I looked over at his side. I cried and cried. I cried more for me than for him. I knew that he was happy, that he was no longer in pain. I curled up and hugged myself and began to rock. I rocked back and forth, like I had done when I was a child. It soothed me. I decided to let them out. I decided to let my tears out. I decided that it was time to cry myself dry, and that's what I did.

Angela arrived. She looked at me. I could see that she was devastated too. She loved Paul too. The three of us had many good memories together. Angela asked me if I wanted a cup of tea. I said no. I continued to rock, curled up in a tight little ball, and cry. She said, "I don't know, Jean. All I can say is if this is what love is, then I don't want to know it. I don't want any part of it." She meant it. She meant every word of it, and I knew that it came from Mum and Dad. I knew that she was afraid to love as I had. She was afraid to let go in case someone hurt her. It was at that moment when I knew that she was afraid someone would hurt her the way her mum and dad had.

My dad had died two years previously, and I hadn't really cared bar one night. I was detached, as was most my family. We weren't too sure how to feel. We were sad, sad that it had ended the way it did. That he had died an alcoholic. I was sad, as I hadn't really ever known my dad. I was sad that he had never tried to talk to me, even at the end. I know now that I mourned a dad that I never had. I mourned the loss of never having a dad in the first place.

But this time was different. This time I was mourning the loss of my love for Paul and his love for me. I was mourning my best friend. He was the only friend in the world who knew everything about me, flaws and all, and still loved me. In fact he loved me more; he loved me more for my flaws, because of what they had made me. He loved the way I had strength amid the pain.

He loved the way I could see things so clearly, how I could see situations so clearly. How I could know how other people felt. We used to laugh about it. I told him that it was because I had been through so much, that whatever they had been through, I had been through it too. It gave me an insight that people my age don't always have. Paul used to say, "You know, people listen to you. Do you know that, that they listen to you?"

I replied, "That's because I listen, Paul; that's because I hear. I hear their pain. I see their pain, and all I want to do is help take their pain away." All I want to do is take my pain away.

The following morning I went for a walk with Angela. As we were exiting through the gates, I turned and saw Paul's car parked in beside mine. It was then that I noticed something I had never noticed before. Paul's car registration was the same as that of my sister Joan's work number except for one digit. The second digit had the number one in it instead of the digit two. Then I looked at my car registration and saw that mine was Joan's home number except the second digit was the number one instead of the digit two. It was a strange sight—one that I will never forget. It was like meeting Paul was very much a part of my destiny, and it was, as he was never to leave my side in truth. When we returned from our walk his car had been removed. I was never to see Paul's car again.

Liz came down later that day and took over, and she was right to; someone had to. She asked me what I wanted to do—the practical questions—did I want to stay for Paul's funeral, or did I just want to go home to her house and rest? I said I wanted to stay. I told her I wanted to say good-bye to Paul in person. Given the circumstances—that he was now back with his wife and family—I didn't know whether that was acceptable or not. It should have been—Paul had separated and moved out—but given that was so recent, I knew that I had to be sensitive to his family.

My sister rang Derek, who told her that he didn't think that was a good idea. He was just trying to avoid any confrontations that might take place between Paul's wife and me. That was natural, I guess, except that Liz was having nothing of it. She told him in no uncertain terms that if he didn't find a way that she would find a way to put this whole situation out in "the papers" for everyone to know. She told me this after. She was quite happy with herself, as she had gotten the result she wanted, for I was allowed see Paul. I was shocked and horrified. It taught me a lesson—never put yourself in a situation where you have to go to the "papers" for anything. While I was very grateful to her for her help, I wished it had been done differently.

The next day, Paul's brothers arrived to relay their condolences to me. It was heartbreaking, but I was so glad they did. One of Paul's brothers was particularly compassionate and understanding. Shortly after, Martin, Paul's youngest brother, brought me to see Paul in the funeral home. While we were there, literally just there, Anne came in. I just turned and gave her my deepest condolences before parting and leaving her with Paul. I had done what I needed to do; I had seen Paul at peace. He looked happy, very serene. It was a beautiful sight.

The funeral took place as if Paul had never separated from his family. I was treated as a stranger, as a distant friend. His immediate family, Anne, and his three adult children knew that he had died with me. It was decided to let his mother know too, so at the funeral she did ask me some questions around his passing. I just let her know that it was very quick and peaceful, almost like he knew it was happening. He had hung in for as long as he could.

My pain stayed for a very long time after Paul died—a deep pain like I have never felt before or since. I didn't think any one person could do this to me, but he had. After a week had passed I knew I had to go back to work. I had worked in one or two of the same companies as Paul had. We both had left our secure permanent jobs and taken up consultancy roles together.

I'm sure some suspected that we got on that little bit too well in work; others didn't take time to notice. We had worked well together as a team, but now we were a team no more. I was on my own, and I needed to go back to work for the money. There was no one else to provide for Christine and me. So that's what I did. I went back to work and acted like nothing more than my good friend Paul had died. I'm not too sure it worked, but I pretended. I was hurting too much to do much else.

The night before I returned to work, I decided to have a little chat with myself. It reminds me of the time when I was young and I stood looking in the mirror. It was one of those chats. I was feeling sorry for myself, so I said to myself, *I know I can't deal with this now. I know I can't mourn you now, Paul, but when I get time in the future, sometime soon, I am. I am going to take a year out and mourn you. I am going to get through this time knowing that. I know that you are not here physically for me anymore, but that doesn't mean I can't talk to you. I am just going to keep right on talking to you like as if you are here beside me, and when I am scared and lonely I am just going to talk to you like you are here.*

So that's what I did. I went to work, pretended I was normal, and went home, cried, and talked to Paul. I did this for a number of months before coming to a decision. I decided one day that it was time to move. I knew that I had no money to do it, but I decided not to think too much about that (Ireland was by now experiencing its biggest recession ever; one of its national banks had just collapsed overnight). I decided that I was going to move anyway. I was going to move for my sanity. I was tired of sleeping in the bed Paul had died in. I took Christine with me house hunting. I decided that we were going to get a house with a garden close by to where we currently lived. We got one and went about moving everything from my apartment into it, just Christine and I. It was the first time I had felt excited in a long time. It was September, four months after Paul died.

When everything was moved out of my apartment, I went back in by myself just to say good-bye. I walked gently over to Paul's side of the bed. I looked at the ground beside the bed where he had died. I cried a lonely cry. The tears dripped down onto the floor where his head had been. I bent down to rub them away and found a piece of paper underneath the bed. It was a piece of medical wrapping from where the ambulance crew had in their hurry thrown it aside. I picked it up and put it into my pocket. It was the only thing I had left as a memory of what happened. Everything else was gone.

I walked out, closed the door, and moved on, just like I always did, just like I always had to. I rented the apartment shortly after, to a fabulous young couple with their whole future ahead of them.

* * *

For a long time after Paul died, I retreated within myself. I went inside and prayed for a miracle. I had no one to turn to. My family was simply too busy and didn't really get it—I was the first to have lost my partner to death. So instead I prayed liked my life depended on it. I prayed for happiness and for a supportive and loving environment. I began to daydream.

Slowly I started to change. I started to see the world differently. All of a sudden—-out of nowhere and out of a deep sense of ongoing despair—every corner, every turn was an opportunity for new and exciting things, people, and events to flow into and out of my life. Every chance meeting became almost magical. I can't tell you how this happened—it just did—and instead of questioning it I "mentally" decided to go with the flow of this feeling, as the alternative was not pretty.

It was at this time when I made a clear decision to give up on my old ways of trying desperately and badly to control the world around me. I decided to have a little faith. I let go of my own internal resistance. I decided to believe in God and his eternal love and strength in everything around me (I just didn't call him God to start with, as the old God I grew up with had no compassion—it only knew sacrifice with no end in sight).

I started to live a life of guidance. I simply had no choice—it was this or nothing, this or addiction. I chose, through some semblance of caring enough for myself, to have something. I chose life. It wasn't long after this when I fell in love again, and I know for sure that it was with Paul's help. I know now that Paul never left my side, and I am eternally grateful for this.

Just as all of this was happening, I was guided to a local lady who was a well known reiki therapist (healing via the laying of hands on energy centers throughout the body called chakras) for a number of emotional healing sessions. It was here where I felt most at peace. After one of our sessions, she turned to me and said, "You know, Jean, you have the most unusual thing I have seen in some time. You have two swords connected to the bottom of your feet. Did you know that?" Naturally I didn't.

Reiki healing was the most outlandish thing I had ever done thus far in my life. To go beyond and say I had swords at the end of my feet was beyond all comprehension for me.

She continued, not put off by my lack of response (which I see as a great trait now): "You know, it's almost as if your feet never touch the ground. You are going to do something to help others, you know."

It was then when something clicked with me inside, and I said, "Yes, I get that feeling too. I know that this is all happening for a reason. I'm just not sure yet what the reason is." I left that day with an eerie sense of what the first inklings of insight must look like.

As I look back over my childhood now, the sensation that she described is exactly how I felt; it's as if I was never "present" when my abuse took place. It was as if I was hovering over my body looking on at what was happening to me. It was as if I was always just a witness. Strange though that she could describe it the way she did, but then again she was also an artist, so I put it down to her creative side coming out. It is only now that I have let my own creative side appear. It is only now that I see the need to.

Here are my few words to describe a friendship I will have for life:
Paul, you are forever in my heart. We are forever one.

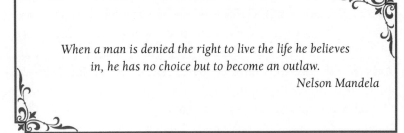

When a man is denied the right to live the life he believes
in, he has no choice but to become an outlaw.

Nelson Mandela

CHAPTER 14

The Standoff

*M*eeting Pierce was the easiest thing I ever did. My sister Angela invited me away for a week's getaway nine months after Paul's passing. It was early 2010, and I was ready by this time to let go of Paul. I knew that it was the best thing for both Paul and me. I knew that he would want me to have my happiness, as I was assured of his in heaven. He was such a good person in every way that I was assured that he had walked his own way there.

By this time, my sister Angela was also looking for a nice man, by now for a long-term relationship. It just so happened, though, that I was to meet mine before she met hers. On one of the nights out, I bumped into Pierce. Quickly we found out that we had a lot in common, and so we merrily chatted all night long. Pierce had worked his way up the corporate ladder to a senior management level. Like any good human resources specialist, I was closely observing whether this position of responsibility had gone to his head! Lucky for us both, it hadn't, and so from that day forth, we quickly became inseparable.

Pierce had a soft outside but a steely core. I loved this about him. I also loved the way he wanted to make me happy, truly so. It was his only motive. He had no other. He was a man of control yet no control. Control in all the right ways, and none in the destructive ways. He yearned, like me, for more. He yearned to live life to the full. It always made him question things, and it was these very things that we had in common.

By June 2010, I had taken another unexpected plunge to move back to my birthplace of Cork. It was a practical move that initially brought me closer to Pierce, but mainly it was to move further away from Paul and our memories together. Finally I had the privacy I craved to mourn Paul in my own way and time. Pierce gave me that time too.

Everything quickly began to fall into place once Pierce moved in with Christine and me. He was extremely relaxed in nature, attentive, romantic, and always around. At first my daughter Christine resisted him, as, like any child, her loyalties lay with her dad. By now her dad was abroad full time, and while they had always maintained contact, I knew that she needed a consistent male figure in her day-to-day life—one who would not take from her dad's precious place in her heart, one that Pierce never dared to take but where he found a place nevertheless.

All was going great. I had every kind of happiness I was looking for in Pierce. It was the stuff dreams are made of. I had finally made it to a place where I was secure, safe, and adored. Yet, I was still waking up every morning with nausea in my tummy. I had spent most of my childhood and adulthood waking up this way. It was only now that I had the chance to truly stop, feel and acknowledge it. I had been too busy just surviving, making ends meet. I have covered it over with all kinds of tablets and distractions, men, alcohol, hectic schedule, etc. But now I was beginning to let it come to the surface.

My tummy was obviously trying to tell me that there was still something terrible going on, but try as I might at the time I couldn't figure out what. It is not until I look back now that I see all the "triggers" that began to take place around this time. These triggers ran deep; they were embedded in my subconscious and in my past. They had always been there, I guess, lying quietly underneath like a giant iceberg, its tip almost visible but the rest well hidden from the untrained eye.

One trigger had been the move back home itself. Memories flooded through my mind, endlessly perpetuated by my proximity to where my abuse had taken place. My one surviving abuser, Jonathon, had remained living close to where we had grown up, with his wife and two children. I was terrified of bumping into him at any time, least of all when I wasn't expecting it. As a result my old vulnerabilities were returning—my childhood nightmares—and as of yet I still hadn't learned how to deal with them. I hadn't put my past to rest.

Another big trigger was my daughter—she was close to seven years old, the same age I was when I stood in front of my bathroom mirror and with quiet determination whispered, "I can't deal with this now, but I will deal with this when I get older." By the time I was Christine's age, my parents had deserted me in almost every way possible, leaving me vulnerable and unprotected from my abusers. I see now that given her age and her innocence, I would do anything to protect her. This was a very big trigger for me.

This kind of childhood abuse was now finally coming into the headlines in every paper and news broadcast. Clerical and nonclinical sexual abuse was finally being confronted. In doing so, it appeared that those in positions of leadership and responsibility on occasions misinterpreted the relationship between those pedophile priests and their victims as somehow consensual.

I know that in the aftermath of my abuse I had rightly or wrongly questioned whether my family had contextualized my abuse in this way. Had they somehow thought I had encouraged my abuser or that I somehow knew what I was doing? This unanswered question, the continued silence and lack of support by my family, fostered terrible guilt and a feeling that I had done something wrong. No one have ever reinforced with me that it was normal to be devastated by what had happened to me or that I had done no wrong.

As I began to reestablish a close relationship with my sisters who also lived close to home, my need to address the impact of my abuse and the way my family—particularly my sisters—both perceived and dealt with it was becoming a major preoccupation with me. In fact, for a time it consumed my very existence. I became obsessed with every move Angela and Liz made; I was hoping if I could understand them, then maybe I could begin to understand me too.

*   *   *

Approximately a year after my returning home, in the summer of 2011, my sister Liz asked me to arrange a family meeting. It was to be on the topic of our uncontrollable mother. She was upset, I could tell, and so I did as she requested. I called my two sisters still in the country, Angela and Joan, and convened a meeting without our mother in my home on this very topic. Mum had just turned seventy and was by now completely dependent on Liz's every move, even more so since Dad's passing.

Liz started out by telling us she had been to counseling with regard to Mum, and before she could go any further she burst into tears. She was stressed, and to her mind, it was largely due to this. After a few minutes she calmed down and continued in her quest for our help. The counselor had inferred that it was unfair of us to ask Liz to carry our mother all on her own that it was for *all* of us to take responsibility for our mother. Liz had referenced this before, but I guess on this day she was at breaking point. We could all see that, and it was heartbreaking to watch.

We went through all the logical and fair options available to us. One of my sisters and I kindly suggested that maybe it was time for Mum to move back home into her own house. It had become vacant again, having been previously rented out. We also suggested that if this was not feasible, then maybe it was time to sell Mum's house and buy a newer smaller one closer to us all so that we could do daily visits and checkups on her while facilitating her back on a path to becoming independent again.

Liz shrugged off all these suggestions, telling us that there was only one way to deal with this. It was for us all to take Mum into our homes more often to give her a break—specifically more at the weekends. Liz thought that Mum was incapable of independent living or being left alone. She may have been right, but in my view that was because Liz had let her become too dependent on her.

I had regularly been taking my mum out for dinner as a way of spending time with her. But it stopped when I eventually realized that the whole dinner ended up being around Mum and her ability to behave or not. If she did behave, then it was a relief, but not in a way that made you enjoy the evening with her; it was just a relief when she went back home to Liz's in one piece so that she and her family could enjoy their evening too. But if she didn't behave then anything could happen.

On one such night she had an accident (toilet related) as I was trying to get her to bed. This was a turning point for me personally, but Liz showed little sympathy to me upon my relaying this story to her. In fact she made clear from the onset her view: "If you can't control our mother, then you deal with it by keeping her in your house overnight, and whatever happens, tough—it's your own fault." Not Mum's then? Interesting, was I to manage my mother from the privacy of her bathroom where she would sneak a sip or many from her "water bottle" unbeknownst to me?

Around this time I had arranged to collect her from my sister's house a few hours after my sister had left for a break—without Mum. When this happened, Mum would turn to drink to hide her feelings of abandonment. Little did she realize though that the reason she was to be abandoned in the first place was because of her ongoing need for drink.

For my mother, drinking on top of her daily medication was dangerous, particularly first thing in the morning on an empty stomach (diet always reigned the start of every day). It turned out that in this instant my mother had hit her head on something, which of course she denied—the doctors told me she had—and the end result had been a shock to the heart as would naturally be the case. She was released after a day after been given the all clear. When I called Liz, she was devastated to know that in her absence my mother had to be hospitalized. This very thing did not reflect well on me.

Clearly my mother was "acting up," particularly in Liz's absence. She had always done this to get attention. Years ago it had been to get attention from Dad; now it was Liz. She craved attention from years of having been ignored by Dad. She was right to crave it; it's just such a pity she never did anything constructive about it. This "craving" was something my mum had taught most of us except Liz. The strong one, Liz, has never craved such a thing. And this was something she was very proud of. She just gave and gave and gave.

But now at last, after many years of the same thing, Liz was finally feeling the pressure of this dependency Mum had on her. Dad had now been dead four years, and to be honest the impact was devastating on her and her family. Her kids and her husband were not getting the attention they deserved as she said. However, the one little snag in all of this, which Liz never relayed to the counselor, was Mum and Dad's property portfolio.

My sister Maria had informed us all that in the intervening years Liz had remortgaged Mum and Dad's home to the tune of one million within a year after Dad's passing. House prices in Ireland at the time were soaring, and so this was seen as a conservative figure given the spaciousness of the site and proximity to the city. It had been completed while Shane, Liz, and their family had taken Mum away to Canada for the Christmas period following Dad's passing. It was their way of keeping Mum's mind off Dad's anniversary Mass coming up, they said. But in reality they had convinced Mum to give them one of the few pieces of financial security she had left in the world.

So to my mind, the only thing preventing Liz from imitating this process whereby Mum could be slowly weaned back to independency had in truth more to do with her and Shane's ongoing dependency on Mum financially. Had this not been the case, my mum as a topic of conversation such as it was would have never been necessary. As siblings, we all knew this, and that was why we were happy for

Liz and her husband to take good care of Mum, which they did very well.

So it was in this context that Liz's adamant suggestion of taking an uncontrollable Mum anytime my sister needed a break was no longer acceptable to me. I also believe now that my reaction to Liz's request was also motivated by the emerging anger and resentment because my mum and my family were not there for me when I was at my most vulnerable and alone.

So without warning and in mid-flow of Liz's suggested solution, I turned to her, looked her directly in the eye, and coldly said, "Do you see that couch over there, Liz?" She looked perplexed but gave a small nod. She was in shock, I could tell. I pointed to the big red cushy couch behind us and continued, "Well, if my mum was sitting on it here and now, it would be my problem and only my problem to get her off it." I took a deep breath. I couldn't believe I had been so rude! My two other sisters just looked at me in shock. All were in shock now, me included. I guess the fight in me was starting to come out.

Liz looked at me and said as graciously as she could, "That's fine, Jean. If you can't accept this, then that's okay too." I could see that she was upset with me, but she held it together enough to bring the meeting to a close and depart on amiable terms. My other sisters let her know they would help her out anytime.

I apologized to Liz shortly after this for the way I had expressed my anger. It was then that I calmly outlined the truth as I saw it. I told her that by not dealing with things we were accepting the unacceptable—by unacceptable I mean that it was by now obvious to all my siblings that my mother was drink dependent, and by ignoring this and not confronting and dealing with, we as a family were only enabling her dependency to become worse not better. To me this—the approach of accepting the unacceptable—was no longer an option.

I did, however, let her know that if she ever wanted to deal with Mum and her issues the right way, through confrontation and external intervention, then I would be right beside her. Otherwise I told her that I couldn't help. Liz did not engage with me thereafter. I guess I was finally getting to a place of no longer feeling guilty for having expectations of my mother that were beyond what my siblings saw as reasonable.

Sometime after this day I invited Liz on a shopping trip. It was in an effort to make amends over our disagreement. I had noticed that after it she had stopped calling me; maybe there was no need to if I couldn't help out with Mum. But I didn't know this for certain, so as a way of ensuring that we didn't lose contact I organized a girl's day out. As I had been away most of my life, I enjoyed these days out no end. It was a chance to make up for lost time, or so I had hoped.

On this particular shopping trip day, my sister Joan just happened to join us at the last minute. She called me and I invited her, and so off we all set. Liz agreed to collect us from my house (she liked to drive, as she told us—all her other sisters—that we were not good drivers and not good at cleaning or good at mothering; the list goes on). I sat beside Liz with Joan in the back.

I was chatting aimlessly when I happened to mention Pierce's recent travel plans, mostly to the States. That triggered a story from Liz. She started to tell me about Shane being in Chicago and how he had ended up in jail while visiting his brother. I was startled. I have never heard this story before. I never knew of anyone being in jail before, so I was intrigued. I asked for her to tell me more.

She started out by asking me if I remembered the time when Shane helped his brother, John, out financially recently on the launch of his artwork. I nodded by way of saying I remembered. His brother was indeed a great painter. I had seen his work and thought it was fantastic. I was really getting into the thick of the story; my ears were peeled for every bit of detail. She told me how Shane had decided to go over to John at the time for the weekend to visit.

For some reason she was unable to go, which I thought unusual but said nothing. I was enthralled: a weekend in Chicago without Liz by his side; that I thought was a miracle in itself. They never went anywhere without each other. She continued by saying that Shane arrived at his brother's apartment complex one of the nights after

John. He was seemingly very drunk and a little out of order, so to speak. She said he had gotten just inside the security gates on foot before he got arrested by the cops and jailed for disturbing the peace.

The neighbors must have called the police, she said. She then went on to tell me what I thought to be the guts of the story, how the American judicial system is very different from ours and how disturbing the peace over there is dealt with very differently from disturbing the peace here in Ireland. This was something she told me she had learned in all of this. I continued to listen intently.

She explained how Shane in his drunken state was allowed one phone call, so naturally he called John to ask him to help him out of jail. John for whatever reason instead of helping Shane rang Liz to let her know of Shane's drunken state and how because of it, he was now in jail. He then asked her what she wanted to do about this. It was midnight or later in Ireland, so she said she didn't think twice and told John not to worry about it, that Shane would surely sleep it off and everything would be grand in the morning. In Ireland this would be the end of it, because normally the next day you are released. However, in the States, different rules apply, as Liz was about to find out.

The next day when Liz had not heard from Shane, she naturally began to get worried and called John again to find out where Shane was; she found out that he was still in jail. Shane at this point got moved to another jail and so was able to make another call—this time to Liz directly. At this point Liz said that she had to organize the next flight to Chicago and work her way from one police "precinct" to the next in order to get her husband released.

The story was so unbelievable to me that throughout I couldn't help but ask lots of questions and express my extreme shock and dismay that Shane's brother could not find it in his heart to help Shane in his release from jail; after all, he had done for him. Liz calmly concurred. She didn't seem in any way put out, nor did Joan, who said absolutely nothing behind me. It was not until many days after that I realized that Liz didn't expect me to ask so many questions; that has always been my downfall.

Eventually, two hours later, we got to our shopping haunt. On parking, I suggested that we eat and relax first—as it was close to lunchtime—before we made our usual dash around the shops in search of bits and bobs. We each had a glass of wine and a nice bowl of pasta and again chatted aimlessly. At the end of the meal, Liz stood up to go outside for a cigarette. It was too cold for us to go with her, so Joan and I stayed in our seats while Liz walked out through a glass door directly in front of us and from behind it lit up, turning to smile and shiver at us as if to say we had made the right choice by staying indoors.

The door had barely closed when Joan from behind her glass of wine calmly said, "That story Liz just told you about Shane in Chicago is a complete lie. Here is what really happened that day, and I know because she called me that day." My mouth hung open—then when I realized that Liz was looking at me, I did a quick recovery. I know, though, that she knew what Joan was saying to me; I could tell she had copped it. Joan then told the real story in her own words. It seems that Shane had gotten so drunk that he had completely run amuck in John's apartment, so much so that it was John himself who called the cops to have Shane arrested. John was so upset at the upheaval and pandemonium that Shane had caused to him and his family that he refused to do anything thereafter. John told Liz this and said that it was the real reason why she had to drop everything and go to Chicago to save her husband.

It took a long time after that day for my jaw to close. I couldn't believe that my own sister could lie about something that wasn't even a reflection of her, but I have come to realize that to her Shane is a reflection of her; he is everything to her, where her parents were not. He was there for her when they weren't, and that builds a loyalty like no other kind. It did, however, change the way I saw her from that day forth. I was beginning to see her damaged childhood and how it had impacted her.

The final trigger showing me the extent of unease in my relationship with Liz came in the form of a day trip to Dundrum in Dublin. It was a reel-by-reel replay of my youth when I would be sent into town continually to collect my drunken dad from the pub. It was up to me to cajole him home—a difficult task for anyone, but particularly for a child. But this day it was not for me to cajole anyone—I was in no mood.

My sister Liz had mentioned that they were opening a new shop in Dundrum. She mentioned it casually, without an invitation to join her, so I didn't think I would end up meeting her. I suggested to Pierce that we bring Christine down and make a day trip out of it, stopping for lunch on the way back. By this time Christine had just turned seven. Her loving and carefree personality was coming to the fore. Everyone adored her, her aunts and uncles, her cousins, her friends, and her school. She was finally beginning to flourish under a roof of stability and freedom of expression, which both Pierce and I always encouraged.

We were barely inside the shop's door when I bumped into Liz and all her family. It happened to be the official opening day, so there was music and a sense of excitement in the air. Liz thought this an opportune time to ask me to take her kids home with us, as she just knew her husband was going on a drinking binge that day to celebrate the opening, so I kindly agreed. I had no issue with this. I was happy that she was protecting her children as much as possible.

However, Shane couldn't wait any longer, and so he suggested to my partner Pierce that they go on ahead and have a pint or two while the women finished off their shopping. An hour or so later, we ladies rejoined them. As soon as Shane heard that I was bringing his kids home that day, it was a cause for further celebration. He could drink all he liked and for as long as he liked. It was like all his dreams come true. He turned to buy Pierce another pint, which Pierce kindly accepted.

I began out of nowhere to get that edgy feeling that I was now used to listening to. That edgy feeling was Shane. He reminded me of my dad. He was nice as long as you were nice about going along with him. I decided to sit down with the kids beside a pool table and waited patiently for Pierce to finish his pint so that I could drive him and the entire pack of kids home. But before I knew it, within

minutes, Shane had ordered another pint for Pierce. Out of nowhere
I blew a fuse.

I stood up, gathered all my strength, and walked up to the bar
where Shane, Pierce, and Liz by now all were sitting, laughing, and
talking. I turned to Pierce—I really wanted to turn to Shane or if it was
my dad then my dad—and said in a very loud voice, "I am leaving in
five minutes, not even a second more." Pierce went red in the face. He
didn't know where to look. He had never been treated this way before.

He didn't see what I saw—an alcoholic at his most manipulative,
a codependent wife sitting graciously by his side, and two kids sitting
waiting like their whole life was going down the sink. But I did. I saw
that nobody cared what happened to those kids that day. This was
routine for Shane and for my sister, but it was not a routine yet for
their children. I could see in their eyes, the very look I used to have
as a child, waiting and praying for their daddy to finish up that last
pint that he never would.

Pierce turned and said, "We're going now in a few minutes, hon,
relax."

I stood my ground. "No, we are not. We are leaving now this
very minute."

I turned to the children and told them to get their things ready
and to come with me to the car; that I was going; that I had had
enough. They each got up and followed me to the car. Liz met me at
the car; she could see what had just happened. She turned, looked
me in the eyes, and said, "Sorry."

I replied, "I'll be fine, Liz, once I am out of here, but for now I
will not be happy until I am." Pierce came out and sat in beside me
in the passenger side in a very big huff. I knew that he was right to
be annoyed. He rarely went to the pub. It wasn't him. He only went
when there was cause for celebration, and this to him was one such
day for just two or three pints, no more. I told him I was sorry, that
I wanted to say what I said to Shane and Liz, not to him, but that I
didn't have the courage to so instead I directed it at him.

He remained angry for a time. I let him stay that way. I held
his hand and said, "Sorry" a number of times. We stopped off as

arranged in Thurles for dinner. It was tense for a short time, but then Pierce cooled down so we started to laugh about what had just happened. It was around about then that he too was beginning to see the impact my family was having on me. He knew that I had been unreasonable with him, but at least he knew why. And more important, he knew that I knew it too.

After this event my relationship with my sister Liz quickly became estranged. She made no effort to meet with me to rectify or to try to fix anything between us. She just did nothing, and for a time, so did I.

*   *   *

Around the same time as my relationship with Liz began to fall apart, so too did my relationship with Angela, but for different reasons. It all started peculiarly enough with my partner, Pierce, rekindling, on his move in with me, an old love of his—running.

Over time he encouraged my sister Joan and me to give it a try, which we duly did. It was something new, interesting, and healthy to talk about. We both signed up for a half marathon, and I put a plan in place consistent with my competitive spirit for us to break the two hour mark. It was a tough assignment—one my partner Pierce helped us with. Little did we know how hard it would be! After many months of struggling we finally got our mileage up to four miles (6,400 km), and we were thrilled. One day I arranged for us to run from my home to my sister Angela's, as it was exactly four miles. Pierce suggested that we have breakfast there and then he would come over and collect us after breakfast. I thought this a great idea, so that is exactly what we did.

We arrived at Angela's gate ecstatically happy with our achievement. It was probably our second time ever running this distance. As soon as Angela saw the two of us together, she came out repeating over and over again, "Oh my God, you both are killing yourselves, and I don't know, girls, I don't know if this is worth it." I laughed and continued on into the house. Joan stayed outside to cool down.

Angela continued on in the same vein, so I decided to qualify how happy I was. "Angela, why can't you ever be happy for me? I love this, and this is really good for both Joan and me. It's worth every minute of it for the feeling of elation you get afterward. Why can't you just wish me the best? Why can't you say to us, 'Well done, girls, keep it up'? Why do you always have to tell me to stop, be careful, or don't do this/don't do that?" Angela did not engage with me on the subject further and proceeded to make breakfast.

Joan joined us from outside, and we all had breakfast. Angela started to tell the story of the tortoise and the hare and how she was the tortoise. She didn't say who the hare was, but from my many times hearing this very story it was usually referenced to either me or another friend of Angela's. To me it was becoming clear that even after an honest outburst pleading for understanding and, more important, real support for my new healthy lifestyle, Angela still could only see how she was right—how life was about taking things slowly. On reflection I can't say I disagree with her—I was just craving the freedom to be me and take on a new adventure while being happy for her to be the tortoise.

I continued running—in fact I increased my training—and I think if I was honest it was in spite of Angela's comments. Joan and I did the half marathon in our targeted time. In fact we ran the course a few times in preparation. Physically and emotionally the experience was great for us, and as a woman the added bonus of an even shapelier figure made the whole experience very gratifying.

Notwithstanding my newfound passion for running and general happiness, Angela continually seemed to miss the opportunity to reinforce these feelings and unfortunately instead focused on my loss of weight and general looks in a way that sapped my confidence rather than build it. This happened over a period of twelve to eighteen months.

Throughout this time I noticed how our relationship slowly arrived to a point where I knew that if I didn't compliment Angela within ten seconds of meeting her, she'd call on a trait she had inherited from our mother. She would end up being quickly disillusioned and would commence the usual routine learned from our mum of how "bad" she looked really; i.e., how fat her legs were, etc. She did this until such time as naturally I would intervene and tell her she looked great, and then the whole cycle of focusing on her, to the detriment of me, would start all over again.

Other times she talked for hours on end if someone from town told her we looked alike. On these days I wouldn't need to compliment her, as she would be on a "high" from the compliments of the night before. I got a blow-by-blow account of what she was wearing, the way she wore her hair like mine, how she dressed like me. Days like these were greeted with a mixture of confusion and relief.

On other days, out of the blue, I would visit her and the very opposite would happen. She would look to run me down as soon as someone complimented me in front of her. A good friend of hers complimented my dress one night so much so that she wanted to know where I bought it. She thought it would look lovely on her own daughter. I thought this a great compliment given that I was most likely twice the daughter's age. But as soon as she left Angela couldn't wait to tell me it was her "anorexic daughter, do you know that, Jean?" She had to tell me this a few times as I ignored her for a while. It continued for a few days like this as a result of my ignoring her the first time.

The final straw for me though came on the night of Angela's fiftieth birthday party. A close friend of Angela's, Aine, had organized a "Happy Fiftieth" card to Angela from all her so-called old boyfriends or lovers (she was single at the time and looking for new love). At this point though a strange thing happened—Aine rang my sister Liz to seek her permission to put the names of the partners of all of Angela's sisters on the card too—just for fun, she said.

So on the night of Angela's birthday, Aine herself presented the card to Angela, telling her it was from all the men in her life past, present, and into the future. At the same time we each received a copy to take home with us. Without thinking too much I scanned the card later to see what names Aine had written down. I knew I would recognize most of them anyhow. As it happened the name Pierce appeared before me as one of the names on the list. It stood out from all the others, as for it had been underlined.

My heart jumped a little as I rescanned the card to see if any others had too been underlined, but they hadn't. My stomach gave a lurch, and it was then when I decided to examine the card more closely to see if any of our other sisters' partners had been mentioned, but they hadn't. Not one of their names appeared.

Naturally I was upset but knew better than to acknowledge it or say anything. A few weeks later I casually mentioned this to my sister Liz. She shrugged it off and told me not to worry about it. But this time I chose to. This to me was a step too far. Boundaries had clearly been broken, and it was time to take action.

By now I had had a few incidents with Angela while she was in the same room as Pierce and me—unfortunately, unlike Paul, Pierce was her type—where she would rush to hug and kiss Pierce in a way that made both Pierce and me uncomfortable. It was a replay of my youth hanging around with Angela, where everything was about getting the man's attention at any cost.

After this night I came to a sad conclusion that Angela had talked so much of "my Pierce" that his name was at the forefront of her mind so much so that just prior to her birthday bash Aine had mentioned to me one night that she thought Pierce and Angela would make a lovely couple. At the time Angela was looking for a man just like Pierce—we had discussed this too at length.

I tried my best to confront Angela as nicely as I could. I decided to focus on the "size" difference between us to start with (I just didn't get any further). I let her know that I wouldn't be calling out to her as I felt my slimness had become a burden to her, consuming most of our conversation, and that I would prefer that this was not the case. Unfortunately, though, there was no getting through to her. She couldn't see that there was any wrongdoing on her side.

One day shortly after this decision, I was relaying a few of these stories and my sad decision to end our relationship to my friend Judy. She had also been present on a number of occasions Angela had talked incessantly about my slimness (so much so that she thought, by way of Angela's deathly concern, that I was going to be hospitalized shortly—that was until I told her that I was in fact still 124 pounds and not to worry; I knew I was a healthy weight for my height).

It was she who told me a story dating back to when I had worked for her in her workplace at sixteen. I had obviously triggered this memory in her. She brought me back to a time when we were out as usual and happened to bump into Angela and Joan outside a restaurant they were departing from. During our friendly exchange Judy recounted this lovely story of a customer of hers at the time, the story relating to me also. It went along the lines of this—one day while working for Judy, I completed an errand for her at the shop below where we worked. A lady I had never met before happily chatted with me for a time before I turned and went back up to my workplace to continue with my chores. The kind lady then turned to the man behind the counter, who happened to be Judy's brother-in-law, and told him that she had never seen or heard of such a beautiful girl in her entire life. He of course later told Judy, who in turn told anyone she could think to tell. That was Judy for you—always looking at ways to make you feel fab about yourself.

On relaying this story to Angela, Angela without my noticing casually called Judy over to the boot of her car. She used it as an excuse to get Judy on her own, or so Judy told me. Angela then turned to Judy and said, "We don't tell Jean that sort of thing, Judy; it's not good for her." To Angela, just like our mum, my beauty reflected in her all the things that she thought she was not.

For some reason, it was a much easier decision to let go of Angela than Liz. It didn't mean that it didn't hurt, as it did, really badly. But the decision was still easier. I believe I had never fully connected with Angela, the same as with my mother, given her lack of emotional intimacy. Liz on the other hand was loving and kind, just like a mother should be, in so many ways that I wasn't ready just yet to let go of her.

I think it was around then when I realized that Liz and I were more alike than Angela and I. Briefly in the past I had tried Angela's way—the way of using people the same way as they used her—but that wasn't really me. In Liz, in the part of her that cared, I saw hope. This was what I wanted—I wanted more caring.

*   *   *

It was by then November, and there was little sign of reconciliation with my sisters in a way that I had hoped. The autumn had passed in inaction. I decided to invite Pierce to come to a spiritual healer with me. I told him that I felt like I needed to. I had done so a year after losing both Dad and Paul, and on both occasions I had drawn great comfort. Pierce agreed. It was unusual for him to do so as he had never done anything like this before, but for some reason that made it all the more fun for me.

The spiritual healer was just lovely. He was funny too. We both loved him instantly. On entering his garden he turned to us both and said, "You had trouble on the second roundabout getting here." We both turned and looked at each other and laughed, as that was exactly what had happened. We had gotten confused on the second roundabout to his house. We had gotten lost but managed to get back on track.

I said, "How did you know?"

He replied, "Archangel Michael told me. His message arrived by the crow you see overhead."

We looked up to see a crow circling overhead. With that the crow disappeared. He brought us inside to his little ornate chapel at the back of his home, and before we even uttered a word he had told us both a lot about ourselves, particularly about our personalities. For the first few minutes he directed his attention on Pierce (it was like he had me figured out in an instant) all the while grinning and chuckling to himself. It made us all laugh; his humor was infectious.

He repeated the words, "Pierce I really like you. I really like you." He told Pierce exactly what he was like in a few sentences. "Now Pierce, you are just brilliant. You are a type of person who on entering a room scans it (a vision of Arnie Schwarzenegger came to my mind with his computer eye running through all the permutations and options before him) to see who is interesting and who is not, and within a minute you know exactly who you want to talk to and who you don't want to talk to. You are just brilliant." He roared laughing, his head falling back and forward over and over again until he could laugh no more. I couldn't have described Pierce better myself; this is him to a tee!

He straightened up then as he looked at me. He took on a more serious look. "Now Jean, you are soft, good, and lovely, but by God do you have a fire in your belly and when you have fire in your belly, you have fire in your belly. By God I wouldn't like to get into an argument with you!" We all roared, laughing again as both Pierce and I knew this to be true; we often joked about it. We always make light of my weakness, so making it easier for us to focus on the solution rather than on my fire in my belly.

Almost immediately he was able to tell me of my "abused" past. He went through the times I had been with my abuser, describing the setting clearly, where he lived, and what the interior of his house looked like. He turned to me at one point and said, "You knew this was wrong. I see you. You are turning your head as if to accept that this was something you had to go through. Do you know that?" I nodded but said nothing. He described this feeling, my feeling as a child, very clearly.

It was such a relief to hear these words. It was really only at this point in my life that I truly comprehended what had happened to me in my childhood. It was only now that I fully realized that I had actually been raped repeatedly, that I hadn't been protected, and that I had a right to finally deal with this now—in the safe surrounding of my own home.

The spiritual healer told us that many others had also been abused by this person. Later I showed him a photo of my sisters. He pointed to my sister Joan, who had also been abused by my abuser. He pointed her out and highlighted this very thing. This was both bewildering and a shock for Pierce. It was opening him up to a whole new world, one that defies logic and practical comprehension, one that is only half of the equation. The other half, I know now, is in the things we don't see. It is in our invisible emotional connections (or subconscious), and it is these that are the more important half. I realize now that when we get these in balance, we can achieve anything with our infinite logic and intellect.

Pierce and I laughed on the way home as at one point during the meeting the spiritual healer had turned to me and said, "You are surrounded by angels. I don't normally see angels. I normally just see spirits. But you have two, one bigger on one side than the other."

Pierce said that he felt very left out as he obviously came to a conclusion that he had no angels as the spiritual healer made no reference to his. I turned and said, "That's because you didn't ask for them to make themselves known. I did. I asked for Archangel Michael to be here for me." He laughed, thinking through the simplicity of what I was saying. "Ask and you shall be given; that's my motto," I added smugly.

Before departing and on a more serious note, the spiritual healer was direct in his message: "You need to deal with this, Jean. This is eating you up inside. I can see that. You need to let this out. This is not good for you the way it is." Both Pierce and I knew this to be the case but as of yet, neither of us knew how best to handle this by now imminent emotional release.

Blessed are those who hunger and thirst for
righteousness, for they will be filled.
Blessed are the merciful, for they will be shown mercy.
Blessed are the pure of heart, for they will see God.
Blessed are the peacemakers, for they will be called the sons of God
Matt. 5:6–9, from the Beatitudes

CHAPTER 15

An Awakening

*I*t was December 2011. I decided to go to the doctor to get a low-dose sleeping tablet to replace the two to three glasses of wine I was drinking each day. I knew that I was rapidly going downhill; I was depending on every drop of drink I could absorb. The only thing stopping me from going further was a lifelong craving for some semblance of normality.

I told my doctor the truth, which was that I was having nightmares, that I wasn't sleeping, and that I knew it was related to my childhood. I told him that my parents had been drinkers, and on top of that, that I had been sexually abused and I needed these tablets temporarily until such time as I had counseling. He agreed with me that counseling was the best way, that the tablets were only a quick fix, and that the problem wouldn't simply go away. He recommended a counseling service to me. I thanked him and left.

I contacted the counseling service and was put on a waiting list. I was fortunate I knew the symptoms of depression, I had been in this place before and somehow had always managed to work my way back out. So I waited. At least I had Pierce, my partner. He didn't fully comprehend what was wrong with me, but he was rock solid.

Some weeks later I had my first appointment with my counselor. Surprisingly there was very little focus on me at this first meeting. She explained this was to be the case from the outset. There were new guidelines in place that were there to protect all concerned. They were there to protect the client (me) from ourselves. For example, if I was feeling suicidal then she would need to contact my doctor so that help could be given. I interjected, "I am not going to kill myself." I stopped and thought for a second before I continued through gritted teeth; I was seething again. "I won't because of my daughter. I won't do that to her. I have felt abandoned all my life. I won't let my daughter go through the same."

The new guidelines were also there to protect any child under the age of eighteen at risk of abuse, any kind of abuse. There were many forms, she said, not just sexual abuse. "There is also abuse by neglect," she said. She went on to explain this in detail. I can remember that no matter what she said, I kept nodding inside to myself. This was why I was feeling this way.

She continued. Now I really was listening. "For example," she said, "any children of the alleged abuser may be at risk of the same thing happening to them as happened to you." She told me that if I happened to mention my alleged abuser's name in any of our future conversations even if it was by mistake that in the context of protecting those most at risk she would have no choice but to relay this new information to the social worker's department who in turn could pass it on to the police. Alternatively, I could make a formal statement anytime I wanted.

She wanted me to be clear about this, as she was conscious of what that meant to me, of what that meant to anyone in my position. "Most alleged abusers are known to family," she said. It made perfect sense to me. I understood exactly what she was saying. I began to feel faint. I thought I was going to throw up. My stomach did its usual see-saw flip like a washing machine at high speed. At last I was beginning to recognize the signs—waking up sick in the morning, generally lacking in energy, with mood swings such that I was calm one minute and the next I would explode with anger over the smallest irritant.

I was now anxious. I clung to the sides of the chair. To the outside I looked calm. No one would know anything had changed—just me; I was used to hiding it all inside. I asked her to repeat a detail or two. She did slowly and gently. Soft tears dripped onto my cheeks, and my mascara started to run. I could feel it; I was conscious of it. It suddenly sank in, and I realized that I had a part to play in this abusive ring as well. I realized that I had been neglectful as well.

This was the first time I realized that this type of abuse could still be happening and the worst part about that was that I had enabled this situation by doing nothing. I hadn't stopped either of my abusers from continuing to harm other young unprotected victims like me. I cried at the thought that someone else might have had to go through what I had gone through. I cried that I had put myself into a situation of not helping others the same way others had not helped me. *Will I ever be able to forgive myself?* I thought. *Will they ever forgive me?* Up to this point I had been mourning for my own loss. I had been lost in my own suffering and hadn't thought of anyone else's.

I was beside myself. It was the first session, and already I was tormented with guilt. It was all a haze after that. My body was exhausted. I told her that I would take the week to think about what she said. On leaving she asked if I wanted to come back. "Yes," I whispered. She finished with "You can change your mind about going ahead with this statement anytime, you know. This is entirely up to you, Jean. It is entirely up to you."

I turned and said as confidently as I could, "Don't worry about me. I am very conscientious; I have always been this way. I am not going to change my mind. Once I start something, I see it through. There is no going back now." I thanked her and left.

I arrived back the following week. My birthday had been the previous Monday. I had just turned thirty-eight. I was conscious for the first time in my life of the age gap between us sisters—the age gap between the youngest and the eldest was thirteen years. I had been fifteen and my sister Angela had been almost thirty at the time of my first opening up. This thought began to play over and over in my mind.

I told my counselor that I wanted to make a statement. I explained that I didn't want to leave it any longer, that I was here to deal with this once and for all. She asked, "You do know this could end up in the hands of the police, Jean, don't you? Are you clear about that?"

"Yes I do," I replied. "I'm prepared for that. I'm big enough to deal with this now. I'm old enough and mature enough."

She then asked, "How do you think your family will react to this?"

"They won't," I replied simply. "They won't."

I explained how many years earlier I had gone to counseling. It was some time after my heartbreaking split with Eoin.

"Did you like your counselor then?" she asked curiously.

I replied, "I did. She was lovely and warm but very direct. I liked that. She was like me." I then told her how I went to her for years and of what she had said of my family, that I was to not rely on them for anything. I continued with my counselor, "I know only now that my family has never been here for me in a way I needed, but I am. I am going to deal with this. I have made up my mind, and that is it. The line has been drawn. No more. I am doing this for me."

She thought for a moment and asked again, "Are you sure?"

I said, "One hundred percent sure. We can't do this soon enough. I am not having this guilt hang over me for another second."

"Okay," she replied resignedly, "let's do it."

I know she would have been happier if I waited. She knew what this meant to me. I didn't realize it, but up to that point I had been putting my life on hold. This was the statement of a lifetime to me. I had been waiting all my life for that moment. It was called the truth in the here and now. Finally I was being given a chance to live it.

She took my statement, reviewed it with me, and then got me to sign it. Again she sensed how important this was to me. She said, "I am heading home after this, Jean. I will drop it straight to the appropriate office. I will drop it in myself to make sure it is on their desk for the morning." I was grateful for her concern. I was on a high.

Just as I turned to go she turned to me and said, "You know, Jean, you sound like you have just read everything out of the book. You know everything you need to know. Now you just need to feel it."

I had spent years and years reading about the impact of alcoholism and sexual abuse. I guess I had been so desperate for justification of my emotions that I had forgotten a vital step in the process, which was to feel. I knew exactly what she meant; I was still talking but not actually doing anything about how I felt. It was like I was stuck in second gear. I knew that I had to do something to change as opposed to nothing. I was now as ready as I was ever going to be to feel how I felt at the time of my most hurt and vulnerable. It was time for me to release the pain I had hidden for so long inside.

Later, for the first time ever, I realized that in adulthood, we get what we deserve because we get what we accept. In childhood, we have little choice; we are at the mercy of our parents.

> *All suffering is caused by ignorance. People inflict pain on others in the selfish pursuit of their own happiness and satisfaction.*
>
> *Dalai Lama XIV*

CHAPTER 16

A Breakdown/Confrontation

On Sunday, January 29, I broke down in my kitchen in front of my partner, Pierce. Christine was upstairs happily playing in her room. It was early 2012, and she had turned seven the previous May. She was bright and enthusiastic as always while being sensitive to my every need. I was finally beginning to meet her simple needs too, with unconditional love and attention.

Deep down I knew that I had every right to be upset—regardless of everyone else's circumstances. I was tired of putting everyone else first. In a fit of hysteria, I asked Pierce to call Liz immediately, that it could not wait—it could not wait another minute. It was 11 a.m. on a Sunday morning. I asked him to explain to her that I was deeply traumatized and to let her know that I needed to talk to her about it, it being my childhood sexual abuse.

He understood. He saw how distraught I was, and so he rang her. He returned to let me know that she would be over in thirty minutes or so and hugged me. I loved his calmness, his undeniable understanding of the level of my anxiety.

My sister arrived thirty minutes later, and I made her coffee just the way she liked it. She saw that I was visibly distraught, and she knew that she was there to listen.

I was overcome by the need to tell her how I still felt about my family's response to my opening up about my sexual abuse at fifteen. My head was held high as I made an effort to be calm and kind while I went through how she and my other sister had impacted me beyond comprehension.

I started by asking, "Do you remember when you visited me my first year in college saying that Mum and Dad were worried about me? Did you not think at any stage that maybe there was something wrong with me and that it might be related to my sexual abuse?"

She replied, "No, it never dawned on me."

I questioned further, "Did you not put two and two together when I was anorexic—only just—at Jonathon's wedding. Did nothing dawn on you then?"

She looked surprised. I think she had just put it down to my wanting to be skinny. Yes I did, because I thought that by being "perfect" I might just be lovable. I went on to explain that I did very well in junior (intermediate back then) level school but went drastically downhill after my opening up, so much so that I barely passed my leaving certificate. Again nothing; she didn't make the connection. It was all a complete surprise to her.

I then went on to tell her every last detail with respect to the day I opened up about my sexual abuse and the meeting that followed. It was the first time we had spoken about it since then. It felt great and lifted a tremendous weight off my shoulders. I told her exactly what my sister Angela said. I told her that I would never forget it and at the moment I was struggling to forgive her given the ongoing serious impact it was having on my everyday living. The feeling of not been heard and being let down had persisted, so much so that their subsequent many acts of kindness were overshadowed. I was distraught about this now; I needed her to understand why I was so.

She said that she was sorry that she did what she did to me. She told me that if it happened today she would deal with it completely differently. Good, I thought, she was not trying to extricate herself and was confronting my message in a positive way. This was my real sister, the kind one, an attribute I didn't get to see as frequently anymore given all the personal challenges she had in her life. She turned to me and said in an open and honest way, "You know, Jean, I was so caught up with an alcoholic husband and two kids; I didn't get a chance to think about it again. I thought Angela was handling it. I left it to her. I should have known, though, what she would do. I should have brought you to Scotland with me."

I replied, letting her know that I hadn't expected or wanted her to bring me with her. I knew that she had her own family to put first; I just needed her understanding of their impact on me to this day.

Liz to her credit had seized the moment and had acted in a neutral and depersonalized way. There it was—the truth and recognition I had been waiting for all those years, the truth being that she was too preoccupied and overstretched to comprehend my pain and anguish and the potential consequences at the time. She simply and understandably relied on her older sister to deal with the situation. I was relieved that the truth was finally out.

And while it was out I decided to ask a question that had and continued to disturb me, "You know we could have gone to the police back then. We had enough on my abusers, in particular one of them, at the time. We had two sisters abused by the same man. You both knew about our sister's abuse by the time I brought it up to you."

She added after carefully thinking through what I said, "No, I didn't think to." But as an afterthought and perhaps by way of consolation she added, "Your abuser did get a going-over shortly after that." I knew that this meant he had been cornered and seriously beaten. This was the first time I knew that this had actually taken place, and even then, it was of little consequence to me as I wanted justice and recognition, plain and simple, for all that I had endured, the years I lost, all of them until now.

I then related in detail what Angela had then done to be of help. I described the one session with a counselor in Galway and how this event had centered more around what Angela wanted to do after rather than on my need for help. After that, we chatted some more. It was easy to converse with someone who was generous, introspective, and I thought fully understood my tragedy. I asked her to talk to Angela on my behalf, to let her know that I was upset with her about this and about other things also. After being close we had grown apart in recent months because of her overbearing focus on my slimness and my sensitivity to those comments.

Before she left she turned to me and said, "You know, I knew you suffered from depression all right. I remember thinking that after your baby you were very depressed." I nodded, saying little by way of reply. Later I thought that I was not depressed but rather from the age of fifteen onward had been living with the reality that in my time of need my family had deserted me and there was nothing I could do about it until I was old enough and strong enough to face my past and the related circumstances. To be compassionately listened to, with respect clearly shown for my feelings; only then can my heart truly heal. Maybe my expectations were unreasonable. Was this just too much to expect or hope for now that we were all much older and more mature?

*   *   *

On Liz's invitation I met with her for coffee three days later. Her approach from the onset was very different. It was the controlling Liz I met this day.

"You know," she said, getting straight to the point, "I have been thinking through all the things I have to do, and there are things you should know, things we need to sort out."

"Things?" I queried. I was lost. Was the selfless and compassionate sister of a few days earlier now being motived by her personal concerns and doubts? I had no idea what she was talking about, so I listened carefully.

She continued in an agitated manner. "Things," she said. "Like tell my girls; what exactly do I tell them? Like for example if they were to bump into friends of the abuser on the side of the street and you go pass on the other side, what will they do?"

I replied, "What do you mean what will they do?" I was confused.

I was trying to grapple with what was now happening. She continued, clearly tormented, "Well, do they talk or not? And what about friends of the abuser on our payroll? Do we keep them or let them go? And what if we keep them, and on hearing of this they leave?" I had been caught off guard, as I couldn't figure out where exactly she was coming from, and I was really struggling to take in her message.

More followed, "And what about Mum? Do I have to tell her too along with everyone else?" A large sigh followed before she added, "And what about all our relatives? How do I tell them about this? Something like this came up many years ago, and well, their reaction was not good, not good at all. They are funny with things like this. They will walk past you and me now because I am supporting you in the street with looks of disgust. Are you really sure you want to bring this up again? I am just telling you the truth, Jean, the truth."

Amazingly so, I remained calm. I went through all that she said in my mind and replied calmly, "Of course your daughters can talk to mutual friends anytime they want. I'm sure all concerned will need support, and why would you be letting anyone go? There is no need for that; they did nothing wrong. If they leave you they leave; I can't do anything about that. This is their decision and not yours or mine. I left home at twelve, traumatized, to go to boarding school. Now I see that it was a safe haven away from further abuse. I left, and I am only just back a year. I left everything behind for a reason; I was too distraught at the time to stay in contact, so what my relatives think is not as important to me as it is to you. And finally, about my mother: I don't want you to tell her. I opened up to her at seventeen and she walked away, so she does not deserve to know what I do about this anymore. She plays no part in this for that very reason. Anyway, if you were to tell her she would only do something to cause the focus to move to her; she would become the victim then. She would take from my dealing with my issues. For once in my life I want to give this attention, love, and care it deserves. Can't you see that?"

I paused and took a breath of fresh air before continuing. "I can't help my mother and help myself at the same time. I have to choose, and this time, for the first time, I choose me. I am doing this for me, Liz, for no one else but me. This is to be my justice after twenty-three years, and nobody, even you, is going to stop me." I ended with a sigh. I could see that tensions were quickly coming to a boil, but I knew not to lose it.

But Liz continued, "Well, just to let you know, I have talked to Angela, and she doesn't remember anything. In fact neither of us remembers you mentioning Jonathon. I talked to my family at length, and they can't believe this to be the case either."

I instantly thought she was just doing this by way of avoidance. This wasn't the kind of thing anyone wanted to deal with, especially someone with an image in society to uphold, an image she of all people had worked hard to reclaim on behalf of all of us. So really what she was saying was that what our family, the neighbors, and everyone else thought was obviously more important than my heartache.

I started to feel sick again; something terrible was happening. I could feel my insides begin to die again, like I was back in time living everyone else's lie.

I said nothing. I wasn't able to. I just sat beside her and stared at her and tried desperately to hold back the tears—my childhood tears that she would not let me cry. She was denying me my time now to mourn. She was denying me everything I needed to survive this terrible tragedy. She was denying me along with my unwanted truth. I thought of all my sisters she just might get why this was so important to me—I knew she had heart—but as always there was too much drama going on generally for her to really have time for me in the here and now.

I slowly turned to Liz. I drew on all my strength to maintain my serenity and quietly said, "I am dead inside, Liz; look at me. Look at my eyes. This has killed me. It killed everything in life worth living for. I have tried to kill myself a million times over in my head. I am not worthy of living. I don't know how I have made it this far, but

I have and I am truly grateful for that. I am doing this now for me. This is my time, and no one is going to stop me, not even you."

A few lonely tears dropped off my face. It was Liz's turn to now go into shock. She had reflected on our conversation of a few days earlier, and her priorities had changed. However, I was heartbroken, and here and now I was losing my opportunity to find the truth, deal with my past, and rebuild relationships. Instead I was being pushed back to where I was twenty-three years earlier.

I walked out that day with my heart in tatters. I was so distraught I left my car keys behind on my seat. I had to pull myself together to go back in and retrieve them from the chair beside where she remained stone-faced, confused, and yet angry that I was so emotional about something that happened so long ago. We were now poles apart; her approach had changed significantly, and unfortunately the previous generosity of spirit from both our perspectives had vanished and there was nothing I could do about it. I knew that talking to her further at that moment would have little or no effect; she was surrounded by her own pain (or anger—it's the same thing) and could not see mine.

I'm sure Liz thought she was doing right by me given her position in the family. She was taking control of the situation. She saw that I was losing control by being upset and perhaps to her irrational. So it was her job to get me back on track. That day she was just doing her job; she was doing what we had always done as a family. She was talking through the practicalities of my outburst. It was not personal; we had never discussed our feelings openly, so she didn't think that was what the situation required.

Talking about our feelings was a rarity to us as a family, but I was driven by an inner desperation and sense of responsibility to talk about my feelings, and there was now an urgency to do so. I no longer wanted to do what my parents had done to us or what their parents had most likely done to them. I was breaking rank, I was a maverick, I had mustered the courage, and I didn't care what it took. I was going to allow my darkest and deepest feelings come to the surface.

Somewhere deep inside me I knew it would set me free in the end. It was the only hope I had to end this indescribable pain inside me. The repressed anger that remained with me from childhood wanted its say; it wanted to be given a chance to be heard. I was ready to unleash her, and nothing was going to stop me.

Neither Liz nor any member of my family ever asked me what actually happened or how sexual abuse had impacted my life since. Or asked me to explain how detrimental it was to me, to open up as a teenager in the safety of the people I loved and cherished only to find that there was little by way of support, protection, and understanding. Or how this impacted my belief system and my ability to deal with relationships.

Did no one contemplate or regret the lost opportunity to bring my abusers to account for their actions and be judged by the legal system? There were other victims and witnesses to this terrible abuse then. There was also a possibility that other victims could have benefited from early disclosure. The 1981 Criminal (Rape) Act was in place when I brought it to their attention first in 1989 and again in 1991, but its enactment had not been a consideration.

While my family may have given these questions consideration there was no visible action. I had anguished about them for years, and taking action to pursue them was not a journey I felt I could take without support, until now, where I believed I had no choice but to become single-minded in my approach. I was now determined more than ever that the truth, which had been hidden for years, would finally be heard.

*   *   *

About a week later Liz rang to say she was sorry. She had talked to her counselor and seemingly was told that what she had done was inappropriate. The thing was that she wasn't sure what she was saying sorry for. She said she wasn't sure what she did wrong; she then asked me what exactly it was that I wanted her to do.

What did I want her to do? I didn't have the answer. All I knew was that I was in tremendous pain and her actions weren't helping. To me it felt like I was fifteen all over again. I told her that we would talk again in a few days even though deep down I didn't feel like talking to her ever again. The damage had been done.

For the first time in a very long time, I was completely out of my comfort zone. My emotions were intensely raw from this opening up, and alongside my sisters' clear withdrawal of their love for me I was fast becoming the very thing I had always strived hard not to be—I was becoming unpredictable. This was to be one of my final triggers that would send me over the edge.

A few weeks after this conversation with Liz, my brother Joe, on Liz's suggestion, arranged to meet with me. He rang and asked if he could come to meet with me by way of showing his support. Because the reaction from Liz and Angela had not been what I had expected, I was a little tentative, so I decided that it was best to meet him in a local hotel for coffee instead of in my home. I was beginning to put up a guard around my home, unknown to myself; I was protective of whoever entered my home. I felt that my emotions were not able to endure any more bullying or emotional numbness.

Joe arrived down after work around 6.30 p.m. He walked in, gave me a hug, and said the words, "I just want to let you know we are all here for you." I said nothing by way of reply. I just sat back and looked. I tried not to look too confused. He looked back at me and said nothing. He looked down. He had nothing more to say. His part in this was over; it was all in his body language.

I then suggested that we have coffee. He got up and ordered two coffees and sat back down again. Again nothing—he still had nothing else to say. I had noticed this about Joe throughout the years when we had occasionally met up—he always had little to say. It was like he didn't like to have too many opinions—maybe too many strong women growing up had surrounded him. It was then that he reminded me of Rob, whom I knew to be kind and gentle but emotionally unavailable.

Out of nowhere I started to tell him a little of what had happened up to this point, focusing very much on Liz and Angela's reaction to me: how Liz now wanted me to just forget about everything and how Angela had after talking to Liz sent me one text to say, "Sorry, no excuses," promising to follow up for a chat—"I mean it"—which just never happened. In fact what had actually happened was that I had ended up, out of sheer frustration, calling her to see when we would meet up, and conveniently her phone went dead! Quickly I realized that I was again making all the effort, and I didn't call or follow up with her thereafter; of course, neither did she.

He was thrown by my anger, and his reaction was like that of a rabbit caught in the headlights. He wasn't expecting my focus to be on my sisters. He was expecting it to be on my one surviving abuser. I told him that the police would take care of that, that I was going ahead with my statement, but that the piece that really concerned me at this point was the lack of any contact from my sister Angela and the last memorable conversation I had with Liz where she had suggested that it was best for me not to go ahead with this. His reply was "Well, you know what Angela is like, and Liz, well, she is trying her best."

So accepting, I thought. *If only it really was that easy. But what about my feelings? Did they matter?*

I think I was looking for some verification from him that what happened to me in my childhood wasn't unique in my family—that I wasn't the only one to have endured a life of indescribable pain. I launched into some questions about his youth, how he found his childhood, if he found Mum and Dad particularly ineffective as parents. His reply was to say, "I had a pretty normal childhood I guess ... well, I mean I knew not to rely on them for anything." Anything? Yes, we couldn't rely on our parents for anything ever. We were completely on our own as children. We effectively were parentless.

I didn't pick up on the word "anything" till a few weeks later, so as a result, I continued on in the same vein of questioning, turning quite suddenly over to my sister Liz and to my mind her exact replica of a lifestyle of that of my mum and dad. I asked Joe whether he saw that my sister Liz was living exactly the same life as my mum, just that she was better able (on the outside—image-wise) to deal with it.

I went through all of Liz's children—how one had self-harmed herself for years (similar to anorexia), one was obsessive, and one was depressed and addictive in her personality; another one ran away, like our sister Maria, never to return; another had panic attacks like I had never seen or heard of before for years upon years at night (I was present for them); and another had nightmares about falling down the stairs and killing himself nightly (only to be happiest when sleeping beside his mother, protecting her from "loud" Daddy). I gave him everything I had—I threw it at him like I was a highly paid barrister. He sat before me in awe, with his mouth wide open, and the only words that could come out were "Well, Liz is a great mother; she really worries about her kids."

"Ah yes," I said, barely stopping for a gasp of air, "but does she protect them?" There was no reply.

He couldn't understand where I was coming from or what I was trying to allude to, and to be honest neither was I at the time. It was just that I was so damn tired of nobody opening their mouth to ask the obvious questions (to me they were obvious) that I just couldn't help myself. Again, without realizing it, the walls of silence, ones that had been imposed on me from childhood, were beginning to crumble, and I, the child inside me, was bursting to come out and scream and yell and ask whatever I wanted. *What about the children?* I was thinking. *What about our children? Don't they deserve better?*

I realize now as I look back at this conversation with Joe that I was like a springboard hidden inside a can of worms waiting to be released. Once released, which was the day I confronted Liz in my kitchen, there was no going back. I sprung out of the woodwork, and by God, was I on fire. That fire was my rage hidden deeply inside most of the time—repressed and ignored for all my life—but no more. There was no going back now. The can had been opened, and the worms—my family secrets, all of them—were springing out. I had lost control of them as soon as the lid was taken off.

Joe ended the conversation as quickly as he could by saying, "Well, I just want you to know that you have all of our support; do what you have to do." I quieted then; there was no point in trying to work with the unworkable, so I thanked him. We got up and left. I went home and told Pierce that my brother had said the words "support" a few times but that he had no idea in hell what they meant. There was no action or thought behind them; they were just empty words.

I met my sister Liz for coffee shortly after, again on her invitation. I still innocently planned to re-address what she had done to me previously, but it wasn't to be. My feeling still weren't important enough to spend time discussing.

From the onset, I knew that she was aware in minute detail of what I had said to Joe, as our whole conversation focused on this, aside from a very brief reference to "I don't know why I don't remember you mentioning Jonathon's name." Again I was left with little to cling to in terms of addressing of my raw feelings—other than the clear signal to go away and deal with them myself. There was no way she was going to give me what I wanted, as to do so would mean having to look at her own behavior. For someone who was always more focused on controlling others, this was a step too far.

I realize now that I had just given her all the ammunition and justification she needed to walk away from me (with the rest of my family clearly in her corner)—as naturally she felt that I had gone over the line. She told me this and that she and her children were not to be "touched." I guess I didn't fully realize at the time how much she was truly entrenched in denial regarding why her children were acting the way they were (she openingly talked to me about her alcoholic husband and how she had gone to AA many years ago and of how she was still reading the literature every day, but I guess it was just all talk and no action).

As I look back now I see that she was still unable to see from a point of neutral, that the situation itself was causing havoc in her children's lives, and that she was not to blame for it per se, that maybe it was just time to walk away by way of protecting them, the same way our mother should have walked away from Dad by way of protecting my sisters and brothers and me—that truly there wasn't anything wrong with us; it just had been all down to the ongoing unacceptable situation.

A few days later my sister Joan met me for a run and casually told me of a conversation she had just had with our sister Angela. She didn't realize the hurt it would cause me—no one did—but it wounded me deeply, especially given that the person she was talking about, Angela, had made no effort to make further contact with me. Again just like my mum and dad before them, my sisters still didn't want to come clean.

On this particular day Angela had just casually called in to Joan's place of work, and while there she continually complained about me. She explained to Joan that to her mind I was just bringing this up now for God knows what reason, causing havoc, and when done I would then just move away and leave them to deal with the upheaval in my wake.

This she said to a lady who had also been sexually abused in childhood by the same person and who herself was still working hard to come to terms with it. Joan did at this time point out to me that she knew not to go to her family for support, that she knew she wouldn't get it in the way she needed it. I said that I understood her wise decision in this regard as I hoped she understood my need to deal with my situation differently given the conversations I had tried to have with my family at fifteen and seventeen—for me there remained serious issues between us that needed to be resolved.

As it turns out Pierce and I were thinking of moving, but more to do with his job than for any other reason. But possibly we both knew that given my current impasse with my family, it was also a good time to move. At this time, I was disgusted with Angela's insensitivity and very hurt by her heartless words. The lack of compassion for what had happened to me was bewildering.

Secrets are born out of a need to protect one from hurtful truths. It is denial in action.

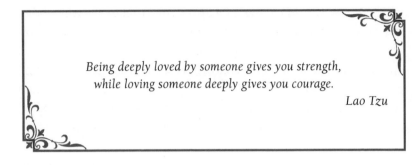

Being deeply loved by someone gives you strength,
while loving someone deeply gives you courage.

Lao Tzu

CHAPTER 17

Last Man Standing

March 2012

*B*y nature I have always been an impatient person and engaged in my work, relationships, and family with a high level of expectation. I think a lot of this "thinking" took place internally as opposed to externally up to this point in my life; hence the reason why I was always in conflict with myself.

While I was deeply impacted by my abuse and needed the support of my family, I was fundamentally not a collectivist. I was not someone who believed that you must be dutiful to your parents no matter what happened to you during your childhood and that you must remain loyal to your family and the church and not bring shame on them. Through my education, my experiences, and perhaps my father's entrepreneurial genes, I had developed by now my own identity. This—my identity—thankfully was supporting me to break free from the pressures to conform to society or family expectations.

I now had a burning need to break free from the pain inside, the pain that I had carried from childhood. I was not going to conform to others' expectations of me any longer. That would have meant surrender and resignation to the fact that I could not change others' sense of ownership, acknowledgment, or responsibility for what happened to me in my childhood and so put this part of my life to rest. The alternative was a very dark place, a place I was not going to go without a fight but a place I was increasingly thinking about as I became more desperate in my quest for the truth and the salvation of the little girl still living inside.

Unlike before, when I would get respite from my past and get on with living as best I could, my nightmare was now all consuming; it never left me for a second. It occupied my thoughts, my conversations with my partner, my relationship with my daughter, and my dreams.

As direct communication with my sisters broke down I started to send text after text to family members. I became obsessed with trying to understand and communicate how our parenting and alcoholism led to dysfunction within our family and how we were still vulnerable to its impact. The "how" of what happened to me and was still happening was such a consequence that I began to challenge our very way of living as a family, our value system, our beliefs, and even our parenting. I was fighting with all the passion I could muster; I had a deep reserve of anger and indignation that I needed to burn off. As of yet there were few tears; I could not get them out. This very thing angered me even more.

My family pleaded with me to stop and return to the old me, but I ignored them and continued on in my quest for the truth in the only way I thought possible at this time—I fought my way there. Around this time my sister Maria joined in, in support of my two other sisters, and texted me to let me know that I was only seeking to further alienate myself from my family and that it would be up to me to work to reestablish relations in the future should I wish to ever have any chance of a family again.

To their mind my family felt that they were being bullied and harassed, and rather than confront me to better understand my out-of-character behavior and the context of my pain and anger, they took it personally; it became an issue of principle, and in that, they found consolation and support in one another. I was clearly out of control; I had stepped over the line, and while one member of my family still gave me hope, generally I was to be ignored and ostracized until I saw it fit to come to my senses.

These were very dark days for me, and the support of my partner, Pierce, was tested beyond all limits. On moving in together I had found his calmness, his deliberate and clear thinking under pressure a source of great strength. Even with this, my constant anxiety over the loss of my family, their lack of support, and the ongoing denial of my truth put significant pressure on our relationship.

During one of my darkest times he had an important business trip planned. On the morning of his leaving I walked in as he packed and calmly suggested that it wasn't a good idea for him to go on his business trip. I knew not to take my cold-blooded anger out on him as he was not to blame, but my body language was stiff and unusually unwelcoming.

The previous evening I had turned to my sisters Angela and Liz one more time with what I saw as the truth—that they had let me down too and that it was time all took responsibility for that. I was finally reaching a stage in my life where I felt strong enough to tell them how this fifteen-year-old inside me had spent every day since that day working hard to stop from killing herself. This opening up had been more significant than anyone or even I could have ever imagined. It was like all the pieces of the jigsaw were beginning to fall into place at once. My sisters did not react. There was no response, no acknowledgment, and no call to check to see if I was still okay.

Pierce knew this, but he calmly explained that he could not cancel at the last moment; a lot of meetings had been worked around him. He was very angry that I was asking him to do so. I reacted angrily back, just the way I had learned from childhood. It took everything inside me not to fling myself out the bedroom window. I told Pierce this in a loud shrill, but given his deliberate nature he had already considered this might happen and had concluded that I would get through it; I guess he knew that I needed to find my own inner strength.

He kissed me good-bye and told me that he would see me in a few days. It was a moment of pure tenderness; he was visibly upset upon leaving. Both of us knew, at that very moment, that our relationship might not survive this kind of pressure. Neither of us said anything; it was just one of those things that went unsaid.

Later that day once I had calmed down somewhat I rang Joan to organize a run with her. She told me that she had seen some of the texts I had sent to Liz and Angela; she said that Liz had called into show her. In the texts I referred to how ashamed they should feel as to me they obviously weren't feeling ashamed—or more precisely they weren't acting or showing "ashamed" to me; in fact, all I could see was contempt and hatred for me. So I interrupted her, asking, "Why has no one called me? Does anyone care what is happening to me? Why is she calling you instead? Does she have something to prove?"

She had no reply to this, but after a quiet pause she said some lovely words to me: "Remember, Jean, the person you are, that lovely strong person; just remember her." I instantly cried and thanked her. This little bit of support—and it was little, but I knew it was all she was capable of giving—was all I needed to keep going in my search for the truth. That evening I sent the following text to my family by way of acknowledging my strength. It was my way of saying that the can is most certainly open, those ugly worms are coming out, and there is no going back.

29 Feb 2012

I am very sad that it has taken me getting to thirty-eight years of age to be able to have the strength to let the fifteen-year-old inside me be angry, very angry with you both for having not protected me. My anger up to this point was at my abusers and Mum and Dad. That thirty-eight-year-old is very sad that she didn't listen to the fifteen-year-old inside, that she didn't help her. I ignored her the same way that you both ignored her, and in the process I have lost twenty years and have been continually searching outside for validation of my loveliness instead of just being there for that fifteen-year-old and holding her hand. I am angry with both of you, and on behalf of that fifteen-year-old that I am now happy to stand by and protect, I make no apology. The wrong is all yours; she is not living your guilt and sick secrecy anymore. I hope this fantastic thirty-eight-year-old has made that perfectly clear.

(Did nobody see the damage? The little girl inside? Could no one see her cries for help?)

Somehow I got the strength to get through those few days on my own. I don't know how; I'm just glad I did. No one showed up at my door. There was no call, no text, and no support. My mum was living less than two kilometers away from me, and still there was no sign of her. There was simply no one—that's how it felt, and that's how it was.

On his return Pierce was welcoming and loving as always, but there was an underlying tension between us that had not been there before. I got the sense that he had remained upset with me for having put him in the situation I did, and he knew that I was upset with him for not having remained with me in my hour of need. This was as heavy a situation as it was ever going to be. Throughout this time, this thought continually visited my mind: "Did no one think me capable of committing suicide?" My strong exterior blinded them all, I guess. It had even blinded me, but not at this time—at this time I knew that I was capable of anything; such was my loss of control.

Over dinner that evening Pierce brought up for discussion with me my need to pull myself together for the sake of my future relations with my sisters. He was thinking long term and was looking at this from a conflict-resolution standpoint. I wasn't! Maybe I was thinking that this situation was in fact insolvable; in those few days I had been forever changed.

My response to his level-headed suggestion was instant. Again the repressed anger, my little girl inside, clenched her teeth with disdain. With unrivaled hatred I hissed back, "Don't you ever tell me what to do again! Don't you ever tell me what to do when it comes to my family. I know better than you in this instance. I know the history. I have lived it; you haven't. Don't you dare ever cross this line again with me; don't even try to go there."

Tears flowed like a river endless in meaning down my face. I had had enough. I wasn't going back; I was only going forward, and if he couldn't see that, then I was going to do it alone. At this stage I had let almost everyone go. There was few left standing with me, but I didn't care anymore. This little fifteen-year-old was coming out, and I simply had no choice but to let her out; she had been locked up inside for too long. I was aware enough of myself to know this. It was this or we both would die. My outside couldn't take the inner turmoil for even a second more.

Pierce saw my desperation and anguish and let me be for the rest of the night. He had never seen me so focused and so very upset in his time with me. That night he got a real sense of how serious this tragedy was for me and for my whole sense of belonging. I was just getting exhausted trying to explain it to everyone. Did no one see how I felt? Did anyone think me deserving of such pain given how my trauma had been dealt with at fifteen, seventeen, and now by the very people who claimed for so long that they loved me? Is this what love looks like?

The following morning, Pierce came to me and gave me an unreserved and sincere apology. The penny was finally beginning to drop. He was beginning to see how childhood sexual abuse and the way it is subsequently dealt with could taint every single good thing that came one's way thereafter. He could see how it was impacting me to that very day; I was still living the pain of my past. He said he understood.

He was angry with my sisters too, but for a slightly different reason; it was, as he said, like they were letting him down too. The reason he said he questioned me was that he couldn't believe that my family wasn't here for me, and therefore he thought that there was something I was doing that needed altering. I replied, "I used to think that too, that there was something wrong with me and not them, but not anymore. They are okay with me as long as I don't react, but I no longer believe that to be healthy in such a serious situation as this. In fact I believe the opposite; I believe it to be totally unhealthy to not react with humanity and compassion."

He said he felt like there was no one to support me, only him, as the ones who had done the damage all slowly walked away, ridding themselves of any blame or responsibility along the way. I was just beginning to see the great tragedy that it was—all of it, every single piece of it, including those who had done the damage. How it was hard on them too. They had been put into a situation of creating even more damage on existing damage; it was endless—damage upon damage with no end in sight.

But I knew I needed and deserved the attention to go on my childhood at this time. I was the person here who had been abused as a child, and my family—the very people who should have been there to protect me—did virtually nothing to stop it; they had a right to know, and I had a right to tell them how they caused me great pain, and again now how they were compounding the pain by denying any responsibility. This alongside my parents' total disregard for me in every way conceivable had left me feeling isolated all my life thus far.

I kept thinking to myself—if only they would tell the truth, then all would be healed as I wouldn't be made to feel like I was the only insane one anymore. The truth could set us all free, because then there would be no need for sides; we could all meet at neutral—the whole truth.

I was delighted to accept Pierce's apology. At last I had found someone who might just believe me. At last I had found someone who would stand beside me while I could get my own strength back again to resume the role of equal partner. I had been weakened, but I also knew that I could use this as a way of strengthening myself up again. I was determined to stand tall from there on in, and no matter what, I was going to tell the truth. I had nothing to lose at this point; I had already lost my family. I had possibly lost them twenty-three years ago; such was the effect of that day on me ever since.

Pierce began to listen to me more than ever. He started to engage in conversation with me, and in those times when he did, I was truly grateful to him for making the phenomenal effort to understand the impact my childhood really had on me. There were times when we wobbled, when our relationship came under enormous pressure as normality would once again throw itself out the window, but each time one or the other was reasonable enough to come back and negotiate to bring all back together again, possibly even closer than before.

In Pierce I had finally got past the wall; I had found a good friend and partner. His love for me was what had won through—for it had been hard for him to see right from wrong amid all the pain. Amid my family's turmoil there was no clear victim; the pain of all smeared that very distinction.

Throughout this time, I had continued on with my counseling, where I found my counselor extremely supportive. I was now at a stage where I had acted out on my feelings, and so our relationship came to a natural end. I think that deep down I was tired of relying on someone else to fix everything for me. I wanted to take control of myself, all by myself. It was time to move on.

As a way of taking my power back, I made a clear decision at this time to turn to writing, enabling me to release my emotions freely and abundantly and as I needed. This approach also allowed me to piece together on paper the sequence in which each one of my traumatic childhood events took place, like putting Humpty Dumpty back together again.

I found this experience liberating, so much so that I wondered endlessly why I had not done it sooner. But of course I know why I hadn't done it sooner. I had been too traumatized by life thus far to give myself any time to get to know my true talents. I had been too preoccupied with my "hidden" pain to make time for anything else.

But here I was, no longer waiting for anyone to fix me. I just needed to be patient with myself, allowing my writings to reveal the whole truth to me in time. In my writings I found solace in a way I had never found it elsewhere. I began to spend as much time as I could at it.

*   *   *

One morning about a month after I had begun writing, my sister Liz appeared at my house. She commenced the conversation confidently, asking me how "my writing" was coming on. She had heard through a mutual friend that I was writing.

I told her the truth: "It is the best thing I had done in a long time for me." I told her that it was "a great release for me." It was helping me find my way out of the unending turmoil in my mind. When all close to me could not understand, this one thing—writing—told me that I had the right to feel the way I did.

I sat by her side and listened intently. I observed her body language; she was back in control again, just like the older sister I knew her to be. She said, a little sarcastically, that she understood that I needed to get a little angry, that it was natural for me to get angry at her. "Sure, where else would you go? Isn't that what I am here for?"

Naturally, given how she had commenced this conversation, I had already begun the process of switching off internally (I was so proud of myself that I had finally learned to do this). It was hard for me to take her seriously at this point, but I said nothing and just let her finish what she had so obviously, after many weeks of thoughts, prepared herself to say or admit to me.

She continued in the same monotone voice with "I think it is best we let bygones be bygones once and for all." She said, "I am very sorry." Instead of it feeling like a sincere sorry, it sounded like she was reprimanding me like a child.

But I wanted to hear more. I wanted "I'm so shocked at myself for treating you the way I have and especially the way I did at fifteen and again just recently. From the bottom of my heart, I am truly sorry for the pain I have caused you. Please forgive me." Instead there was just this halfhearted insincere truth. How denial can kill a loving relationship.

She then added bewilderingly, "I wonder how I don't remember you mentioning Jonathon's name. I just don't know." Again, I was confused as to why she was still repeating the same thing about not remembering Jonathon but thought it best to say nothing. I was thinking to myself, *What exactly is she trying to say?* I knew that my opening up at fifteen had to be serious enough to remember. We both knew that, so what was this "I don't remember" about? It was terribly upsetting to the victim inside me who just craved the truth in a time of grave despair.

By this time, I knew for sure the reason why Liz and Angela had remembered very little of my opening up—on the basis that this was a truthful statement, which by now I believed. I knew that the logical explanation for "their truth" had to be that their childhood/ early adulthood had been just as traumatic for them as for me. Liz had admitted earlier that she was married to an alcoholic with two young children to care for. She didn't have time to help me, and neither did Angela, who was caught up in her own addiction then too. I don't know why I didn't discuss this with Liz. I guess I knew it was not for me to break this information to her. It perhaps would have looked like I was saying it out of bitterness rather than love. I was hoping in time a counselor or neutral friend would be able to help her.

She ended our conversation shortly thereafter by suggesting that we meet for coffee and a walk anytime I felt up to it. She said that she understood where I was coming from. I said nothing in reply. She hugged me; I hugged her back. I was numb with shock. The coldness was stifling.

I realized pretty much immediately after our "nice chat" that we had gained nothing from our interaction with each other. She talked and I listened, but there was no two-way interaction, no honest interchange of views and opinions, and there were no other questions (aside from the reference to my writings). She just wanted this to be over and done with; she didn't want to have to deal with this now. There was too much going on in her own life, and the only way she knew how to deal with all this trauma was by controlling it in every way possible—which meant trying to control what I was thinking. She basically wanted me to forget about it and move on.

And so we were back living the past, one where everything was to be forgiven and forgotten in one fell swoop. There was no time for retrospection, compassion, and kindness, because there simply was no time; yet again, there was too much going on in the present.

For me, though, I finally was at a place where I accepted that I still needed to converse openly about this terrible tragedy and that I needed and deserved to be listened to. For me silence was acceptance of what is; real change required my voice—and it was my inner voice to start with.

After over thirty years of repression of all feelings, I had found my inner voice. It told me the whole truth. It was capable of hearing both sides. It could be trusted. There was no going back.

Finding our inner voice is the beginning of equality; for only when we hear our own voice can we hear the voice of others.

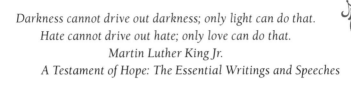

Darkness cannot drive out darkness; only light can do that.
Hate cannot drive out hate; only love can do that.
Martin Luther King Jr.
A Testament of Hope: The Essential Writings and Speeches

CHAPTER 18

A Meeting

July 2012

*C*hristine had just completed her first class in school and was all talk about her summer plans. Living on either side of us were her two best friends. She delighted in spending time with them, mostly circling around our beautiful housing estate on their lovely pink bicycles. She was a natural-born leader, taking charge wherever she could, and the summer was going to be packed full of picnics and further rides to and from the village close by. It was a very exciting time in her little life.

On my side, there had been no contact with my family since my last meeting with Liz aside from the odd organized run with my sister Joan. Fortunately, though, for me, as the months passed by I did—very slowly—accept that my role was to heal myself and not try to change others no matter how noble it appeared. I also began to see that it was this noble stance that also repelled my family from me as they saw me as acting superior to them. So I backed off and focused on me instead.

Throughout this whole process, alongside my writings and the support of my partner, Pierce, I had returned to reiki. In this setting, I found warm comfort—akin to unconditional love and being accepted for who you are—enabling my body to slowly release all of its pent-up frustration/anger without fear of rejection or retaliation.

As each session passed, I felt my body return to me healed. Reiki relaxed me in a way that other therapies couldn't. Its focus was on spirit, which was exactly what I needed, as it was my spirit that had been broken. Reiki seemed to work at bringing about a peaceful space inside me where good decisions could be made. These decisions were so wise that it made them easy to stand by. I stopped going back and forth and instead stood by my right to make choices that were good for me.

Through reiki, I began to understand that pain bestowed upon us like this was not meant to be taken personally; it was nearly always accidental and rarely on purpose. But it was for me to deal with by taking appropriate action to prevent it from continuing or indeed spreading. It was up to me to take responsibility to heal it and then let it go.

At this time as with other times in need, I didn't think to turn to the church for spiritually based healing. The God and church that I grew up with were cruel and unforgiving. I since know differently—I know now that it was a number of Catholic priests in Ireland at the time who gave this impression to those who did not follow their suffocating and controlling ways. But I also knew that this wasn't the time to go back to something that hadn't worked for me in the first instance. Someday I will be happy to return to the church (community-based prayer), but it will always be in the safe knowledge that it is God's laws I follow and not human flawed "image-based" ones (to me this means a structure or person who tries to cover up the truth through silence, denial, lack of cooperation, etc.).

* * *

As my pain slowly subsided I began to focus more on building a stronger and more nourishing relationship with my daughter and a deeper relationship with my partner. The pain of not been able to reach reciprocity with my family and the full realization that I was in fact losing them was still a major source of anguish for me; however, I was beginning to become more impervious to it and started instead to rebuild my life around my immediate family, my healing journey, and my newfound love of writing.

I began to realize how lucky I was to have come through this wall of pain as well as I did, to have a partner and daughter who adored me as much as I adored them, and to have found a rekindled passion and purpose for life like never before; alongside my writings had also emerged a strong desire to specifically help children (or teenagers) who suffered past neglect like me.

With this progress the timing seemed right to once again reach out to my family to try to bring this stalemate to a conclusion. I knew that possibly they weren't ready to hear my truth still—but either way I wanted to "move on." The timing for me to move on was now, and for the first time in my life, I was putting me first. If they could not hear my truth, then I wanted us to part on good terms.

Pierce offered to set up a family meeting that included two of my sisters and one of their partners. He offered to attend it on my behalf. I was very comfortable with Pierce representing my feelings and needs; he had traveled my journey with me and understood my pain and the progress I was making. For me personally I felt that I was not ready to be present at this time at such a meeting, as my emotions were still very much impacted by the need to be heard and understood by my family, and I knew this was clearly not the case.

I knew that Pierce wanted to help me, and I was grateful for his support. He knew that I wanted to bring my conflict with my sisters to a close, that I wanted them to understand that the anger I had gone through and was still going through was a part of my healing process. It had been important that I got it out of my system—it was that or kill myself—as the inner turmoil was too much for me to bear on my own.

Significantly for me and through my realization of the impact of alcoholism on us all, I also wanted Pierce to let them know that I accepted that they may not have remembered my trauma around my first opening up about my sexual abuse as well as I had. I now knew this to be true and had found in my heart an acceptance around this. Finally I was getting "my power" back instead of always giving it away to my family.

Pierce called to arrange the meeting with my sister Liz. When he called her house, my mother, who remains with her to this day, answered. She inquired politely as to my well-being. Pierce replied kindly, letting her know that I was doing well, all things considered. My mum's reply was quite shocking, even to Pierce, who had always remained as neutral as possible: "This must be very hard on you, Pierce. I hope you are going to be okay." Pierce was astounded that my mother did not think it her place to visit me, talk to me, or do anything other than sympathize with the person living with me.

When he relayed this message to me, I did not even flicker with any emotion other than understanding. This was my mother, devoid of any normal emotions that a mother generally has naturally for her precious child, for when we are strong there is nothing we wouldn't do to protect our children, including die for them. But here there was no strength. Instead, the only words to describe my feelings for my mother at this point in my life were those of understanding; she was in too much pain to let go and let live the way we were always meant to be. But on the upside for me at least this was confirmation to my mind that my childhood memories were most certainly steeped in truth, even if all was not exactly as I saw or interpreted it.

At last, instead of questioning my sanity, I had found through my mother's bewildering continued absence in my life that the breakdown that had taken place between us was of her doing and not mine. It was with relief that I understood that my feelings from childhood had validation—that in truth my mother was incapable of real love, that her world was as far away from a loving reality as it could possibly be, and that all that remained was a mist of drink and every kind of prescription drug that could kill the pain in an instant and allowed for no thought, no effort, and no admission of guilt. While it saddened me deeply that this would most likely always be the case—I would want for her happiness instead—I knew that it was up to me now to ensure that I did not continue in this vein.

The meeting convened shortly, with my sisters kindly asking about my health (they just always seemed to miss the personal touch that brings sincerity to this gesture). Pierce explained that while I was still a little tender, I was doing well given that this whole experience had been very distressing for me, and as it turned out for him too. It was his first experience with anything like this. He was well versed in many forms of conflict but had never encountered such emotional damage and pain as what I had endured.

He explained how it had taken him by surprise and how he had to work hard to understand all that had happened to me. He explained how he had wondered many times why people in their later lives would decide to reveal their childhood abuse in such a public way. I was of a similar mind prior to my opening up too; such was the level of my own denial. He said that until he met me he could not understand their motivation.

But now, given all that we had gone through together, we both accepted that these people were denied the support they needed all their lives and so in most cases were very angry because of that very thing. I had come to realize through my journey back to me that anger and passion can be the same thing, just that passion is anger (or frustration) listened to and used in a positive and constructive way. True passion gives us resilience to go the extra mile like no other.

Pierce related to my sisters that he hadn't fully comprehended the impact that childhood abuse could have on an adult. It was only through my pain that he understood that these people had been unable to move on and that a terrible injustice had been done to them, leading them in many cases to be incapable of ever attaining love. It also led to many being incapable of responsibility and accountability (or else incorrectly overresponsible/accountable) in adulthood, and this would continue to be the case until such time as these terrible crimes were dealt with in a compassionate and fair manner. We had both stopped seeing them indifferently and had started to see them as the victims they truly were.

He also explained how he saw and accepted that I needed to go through this bereavement in the way I had and how I now accepted that they, my sisters, might not have remembered everything as it happened. He did, however, explain the implication of their action in this regard, that their refusal to acknowledge my trauma as I remembered it was akin to calling me a liar, and given all that had happened, this was too much for me to accept, for being a liar on top of being sexual abused in childhood was a step too far for any human being.

To me it felt like it was total alienation of my human right, and the right of the child inside me, to be heard both neutrally and with compassion. The reality is that tormented memories like this can never go away until they are believed and acknowledged; otherwise we are leaving the door open to insanity or drugs/alcohol/ sex/relationship abuse.

Pierce continued to explain how this ongoing experience along with other experiences such as living with my parents' addiction had caused me to feel disjointed and isolated for most of my life. My sisters intervened and agreed with Pierce that my parents had not been supportive of my emotional and physical needs, particularly in childhood. They cited clearly that my childhood had been so much worse than theirs—which I do believe to be correct. The problem was that they had concluded during this time—Joan mentioned that they had talked a lot about my childhood relative to their own—that their childhood had in fact been very happy. They felt that they had experienced little or no trauma in childhood.

It was in this light that my sisters then made a significant and supportive statement. They confirmed that they did not deny the essence of what happened to me; if they had previously done so, it was unintentional. Thankfully all now unanimously supported that the details in my mind around my opening up to them were most likely clearer than theirs.

They could do this now knowing that I wasn't there to rebuff them by stating the obvious—that if they couldn't remember all the detail of one of the most traumatic events that could ever take place in a family, did they understand that this was in fact anything but normal? In fact, it is so abnormal that anyone on neutral ground would of course conclude that my sisters were indeed denying to themselves to the level of trauma that they did in fact experience in childhood. For this would be the only logical reason for them "not" remembering my childhood abuse—they were already overloaded by the time my trauma broke.

Of course, Pierce did not bring this obvious conclusion to their attention. Instead he focused on the one thing we both wanted out of this meeting—which was confirmation that my childhood memories were in fact the truth and that I was trustworthy, as I had always shown myself to be. He had figured out somewhere along the line that this was really the most important thing to me. He knew that I was not going to have my "truth" taken away from me by anyone at this point. This truth to me was worth fighting for.

My sisters continued to talk for some time after this. Pierce saw that there was palpable pain on both sides. He had experienced my pain; now he was experiencing theirs. The origins of their pain lay in the fact that while they recognized that today they would respond differently, they had a lot going on in their lives at the time; my sister Angela blankly refused to ever go back there (even generally) again in her thoughts, citing that I knew this to be the case already. She had referenced these thoughts with me on a number of occasions in the past, particularly amid emotionally charged situations.

It was becoming clear to Pierce how my sisters still felt. They had spent their lives since the discussion at age fifteen doing all they could for me in every way possible, and now they were under attack. Their very existence and value system were being challenged, and they could not deal with it. They too were now going inside to protect themselves. Given their pain, they were not ready yet to just focus on the learning from this sorry tragedy. There was a strong personal need for self and family protection, and in order for us to rebuild relations, more time was going to be needed on all sides.

On replaying this sequence of events often in my mind, I have since come to understand and accept that in times of high emotion these are all normal and to be expected reactions, as difficult as it may seem to a victim. More time was needed for the pain that all were going through to subside.

The meeting ended with a commitment by Liz notwithstanding her pain to meet with me and talk through the situation with a greater level of understanding on both sides. So far this meeting has not taken place, but I know deep down that we all remain hopeful that someday it will.

I believe that time and prayer will heal all.

*   *   *

Pierce arrived home three hours after he left, and I met him at the door. When I asked him, "How did it go?" he couldn't answer. He was emotionally drained and physically exhausted. As I had a child-minder organized for Christine, we quickly said our good-byes and drove off toward town for a quiet dinner and private catch-up.

On the way into town, Pierce pulled over the car to catch his breath. He then burst into tears. When he calmed down he said he was surprised at how much he had gotten into character—how much he had felt and understood exactly how that fifteen-year-old had felt that day twenty-three years earlier. He then told me all the detail as outlined above. He had remained neutral, as I had asked him to. He had known to focus on a resolution of the most important truth, not the many truths that I had barraged my family with over a short period of time.

I hugged him and thanked him profusely for being such a kind and loving partner. I knew that I was very lucky to have such support at this time. It meant the world to me. I confirmed to him that as a victim of this tragedy, the part that gave me the greatest relief was when my sisters confirmed that my memory was clearer than theirs; in doing so I felt that the details I remembered could now be seen as real and factual. I was very grateful for this confirmation.

For me it brought my journey with them to a close. It was all I needed of them to start afresh in every sense of the word.

Such was the intensity of my recovery process that I knew that most likely I had lost my family, but in doing so I had regained my sanity—for good. The fuzziness that had been deeply entrenched in my mind and its every thought was no more.

To be or not to be, that is the question.
To be, my final answer!

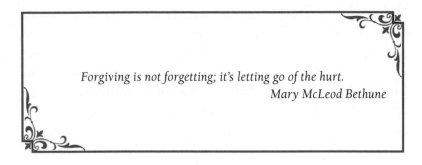

Forgiving is not forgetting; it's letting go of the hurt.
Mary McLeod Bethune

CHAPTER 19

A Simple Message

December 2012

hristmas was on the horizon once more. One day, a friend gave me the business card of a psychic. I thought it a fun idea, so I grabbed it with both hands. I knew deep down that she would reflect back onto me my own thoughts—akin to looking in the mirror. I anticipated that there was good news on its way to me. I had not gone through all of this pain in vain.

I arranged to meet with the lady a week later. I was so nervous the morning of our appointment; I won't ever forget it. She started off slowly—letting me know that she would do a general reading and then we would know where this would lead. I nodded cautiously. She asked me to pick six cards from the deck spread in front of me. I did so and gave them to her expectantly.

She turned them over. I didn't get a chance to see them as she commented, "Well, the good news is that you are nearly there. You only have a little bit to go. So that is good news, isn't it?" I nodded as she continued, "That and you have a long life ahead of you. I'd say till your late eighties at least—maybe even ninety." She smiled. She was lovely—chatty, bubbly, and direct. *Another one like me*, I thought.

She took the leap, "Well, thank God you have left everything behind. Well behind. I hope you don't mind me saying this, but you were a bit of a doormat, weren't you?"

My whole body relaxed and I laughed. "Yes, the very thing."

"Well," she continued, "whatever you do, don't go back, or no matter what I will find you and hit you myself." She asked me where I was currently living, and I told her. She said she wasn't joking; no going back. More laughing … I was at ease with her. She was so natural it was hard not to be.

"Now your current boyfriend and you will be together for a long time." She was just getting into her stride, and I started to cry. "What's wrong?" she queried while adding quickly, "By the way, the tissues are there beside you; they are always needed."

I bawled, "That's such a relief."

She was curious and asked, "Why are you so worried about your partner and you?"

"Because until now I didn't realize it, but maybe I was always fearful that he would die young, like Paul. I was afraid I would lose him before I was ready to."

Well," she exclaimed, "that's not going to happen now, so worry not. Life's way too short for that. Now mind he is a businessman, isn't it? So don't expect him to be sitting around waiting for you at home. He will always be up to something, but it will be good something."

She went on about Pierce for a little while, explaining in detail how much he loved me. How it was an honest love—direct from the heart—and for me it was the same in return. She said she liked everything about him. "He is a good soul."

I said, "Yes, I know—I feel very lucky."

"Well," she replied, "don't forget what he is getting. He is getting you. Your aura is very soft, very soft indeed. Know that he is very lucky too." This was the second time a psychic had told me I was very soft. I knew it was good, but I also knew that I needed to toughen up.

"Now I also want you to know that you have a very close bond with your daughter. Yes indeed. You are very protective of her, and she is of you. You adore her, and she adores you. You will always have this bond. You are a very good mother, you know?"

I was delighted. The positive feedback was just great. I was really getting into the lightheartedness of it. She finished with "She can move in and out of the spirit world, did you know that?" I nodded. I knew my child to be extremely intuitive. By then Christine was wise beyond her years, almost always on hand to dole out some clever little piece of advice just as it was needed. "She still has it," she continued. "Children her age can lose it, but she still has it, so this will be good for her. She is sensitive to you in a way that is just lovely, like when you say you have a headache she knows intuitively the real cause of it and she hugs you and touches you for a while to make you feel better. She gets this from you. Do you know that?" Again I nodded. I was beginning to realize that I had this gift too and that like many other children out there I had lost it for a time, but now I was finally getting it back. I was coming back into myself. I was almost there!

"Does your daughter dance or something?" she queried then.

"Yes she does. She loves Irish dancing. She practices it a lot."

"And did she win a trophy or something recently?" she added.

"No," I said, but before I got time to finish, she said, "Well, she should have. Your dad was there with you at the Feis (Irish dance competition). He loved it, and he loves to watch her dance. Let her know that. He is very proud of her. She is very good. She will win soon." I laughed at this very statement. Christine had danced her heart out at the Feis the week before, and both Pierce and I had come away thinking she had deserved a trophy. She had been a joy to watch. I never thought I could love watching Irish dancing at much as I did on that day. I had told her this, and I had told her she had shown big improvements on her last event in which she had also won a placing medal; I wanted her to know that while her placing may not have improved, her dancing had. It was all she needed to keep her motivated.

The lady continued, "Tell her to keep at it. She is also bright, so don't worry about her studies—she will fly at anything she sets her mind to." Christine had just been diagnosed with weak auditory skills, but I noticed that since we had identified her particular weakness and in doing so worked hard together to overcome it, she had come on in leaps and bounds. Obviously there was nothing wrong with her intelligence.

She changed the subject, "And you will not suffer from depression or anything like that, not like your mother. You are going to be very happy once you get your confidence back, do you hear me? You are nearly back to where you were before this. You understand, don't you? You are nearly there. Hang in and keep going. Your happiness comes from inside, deep inside. I see that. You are so very close. Keep going.

"Now is there anything in particular you want to ask me? By the way, your dad is sitting beside you to your right. His hand is on your shoulder now, and he is kissing your cheek."

More tears! I didn't think I could get so emotional about something so simple, but I did because her words were just so beautiful and I was beginning to understand that life was as simple as this. This very thing—pure love—was everything and the only thing. My dad had never kissed me like this while alive. It was as if one of my big wishes from childhood had finally come true.

"Yes," I popped in. I cleared my throat and said what I had come to say (I was finally getting my chance to forgive in a way I longed for—I was able to sense this now). "I want him to know that I forgive him. I want him to know that I understand even though I don't understand it all yet."

She replied, "Yes, he knows; how long since he passed away?"

"Five years," I said.

She continued, "Yes, he is ready now. He wants to tell you that he is so sorry for not being here for you in the way that you deserved. He wants you to know that he knows that now. He knows that he was verbally abusive and neglectful, and he is so happy that you forgive him. He says that he is not deserving of your forgiveness in the way that you have always given it. You always treated him with respect and love, and he would like to say thank you for doing so. He also wants to say thank you for being at his funeral, that he knows not every one of his children wanted to be there, but he knew that you did (this is true—one sister in particular did not want to attend). He knew that you loved him no matter what, and he is grateful to you for that. He also wants to let you know he is kissing you now to wish you happy birthday. Your birthday is soon isn't it?"

"Yes, it is," I answered heartily.

"Well, he wants you to know that he will be with you on your birthday. He says that he loves spending time in your house. It's so peaceful and quiet, and when you leave your partner downstairs and go upstairs, he goes up with you and sits on the bed beside you. Do you light something?"

"Yes," I replied. I light incense while meditating/stretching.

"Well, he loves it. Is it okay for him to continue to visit?"

I smiled, "Yes, absolutely. I would love him to. I feel him a lot."

"He knows," she said, and she let me know how I would know it was my dad.

I asked her, "What was my dad's childhood like?"

She replied, "You know back then they used sticks a lot."

I queried further, "Both or just his dad?"

"I get the sense that both were abusive," she replied, "mentally and physically."

My dad spent so little time visiting his mother in her later years. I used to go with him but it was a rare treat for me, and as a grandchild, I loved her. My dad worked full time from the age of thirteen; like many his age he didn't get a childhood, so to me this explained why I didn't have one either; no one knew to give me one.

"And my mother's background?" I queried.

She said, "There were mental health issues in her family background, but back then this could have simply been depression." She told me that my mother was secretive about this. She confirmed only what I had already guessed, that there was unresolved issues in my mother's background too and very much along the lines as she had outlined. Both of my granddads had passed on by the time I was born. I was never told how either one passed away, but I sense that there was great sadness around my mother's dad's passing in particular. It was in the way his children, my aunts, took such good care of their mother in her later years. It was as if they felt sorry for her.

She continued, "Your dad also wants you to know that he is extremely proud of you. You have had to make tough decisions of late—the hardest one you will ever have to make, and he wants you to know he is so proud of you for doing so."

"Thank you," I replied. "It's great to hear that."

"My advice is that you keep on disconnecting," she said. "Your family will come to visit you. Listen to what they have to say, as they may change how they feel about you; otherwise keep going and don't look back. Somehow you managed to get to here, but there must be no going back. You are now sitting on the wall looking back and looking ahead, and I am asking you to jump. It has taken you a long time to get here. To go back would only hold you back from your future, and you have a lot to do. Do you understand? You are doing right by you, and that is the right thing to do."

"Good," I said. "Because I hate doing this. It really isn't me. I hate walking away and leaving behind such pain. But I know it's the right thing to do."

She nodded and said, "Yes, it is okay. It is okay to mind and protect yourself from people whom you feel do not support and protect you." She then turned to my dad, who was still there, and said, "You know that your dad guided you to Pierce. Do you know that?"

I replied, "Yes, I know. I wrote a letter of thanks to him."

She said, "Your dad is saying good-bye now and that he will be waiting for you in your car when you leave here. You will both journey back home together."

"Now let me see," she mused, not even stopping for a whiff of air. "Are you thinking of going back to study? Is it counseling or something like that?"

"Yes," I sang with glee. I had been thinking of it a lot recently. In the past two to three years I had looked into it a few times but was always putting it off.

"Well," she said, "you will fly through it and whatever else you do, like the book and play, etc., and specifically whatever you do will be to help children and teenagers."

"That's fantastic news," I replied. "I am so delighted, as that is what I have done. I have just finished writing a play. It is a satirical one, of my family situation. I did this on purpose to keep me laughing while I'm writing this very serious book."

She added, "I see you writing a series of books, and it will be easy for you—like this one. You are going to be very busy, you know? Lots of cogs in there, and just as the Einstein saying goes—you don't have to remember everything—just write it down." Again this made me laugh as so many ideas were flooding through my mind that I was having difficulty remembering everything.

She then said something curious: "By the way, are you thinking of having another child?" I smiled, knowing that at times I wanted another child while also thinking maybe it was too late.

She continued, "Because if you're not, then you need to have protection in place, as there is another one waiting for you. But know that the choice is yours."

I instantly thought, *The Catholic Church and, more important, the women of Ireland could do with hearing those words "It is your choice."* (And the choice to be a woman priest and the choice to be divorced and the choice to be in a homosexual relationship and the choice to walk away; it is not for *anyone* to take choice from us.)

Our conversation came to an end shortly after this. I had just one question left (this is so me). "Are there evil nonhuman spirits out there as well as human ones?" I asked.

"Yes," she replied calmly. "It's like the Nintendo game where there are all different levels, and young teenagers need to be aware of the dangers around this as they can sometimes think they are communicating with someone nice. But this is only a trick allowing the evil spirit time to manifest itself into this world."

I replied, "So don't give them the time or space and all will be fine."

"Yes," she said, "people need to know what they are doing when communicating with spirits, particularly on Ouija boards; otherwise they could find themselves living with an evil spirit. This can ruin many lives."

I knew by this statement that if we can so easily attract into our life evil or negative spirits, then too it must be true for the opposite— if we really want to attract positive spirits or beings into our life we can do this just as easily.

We hugged then, and I left on a high. My life really was doing a 180 degree turnaround, and mostly for the better.

I know now that I am neither angry nor alone. My words are simply for expression. They are an expression of the truth. They tell to me that it is I that am sane, it is just my world close to me is not. They tell me that my feelings are normal; it's just the situation I find myself in is not.

> *Do not believe in anything simply because you have heard it.*
> *Do not believe in anything simply because it is spoken and*
> *rumored by many. Do not believe in anything simply because it is*
> *found written in your religious books. Do not believe in anything*
> *merely on the authority of your teachers and elders. Do not*
> *believe in traditions because they have been handed down for*
> *many generations. But after observation and analysis, when you*
> *find that anything agrees with reason and is conductive to the*
> *good and benefit of one and all, then accept it and live up to it.*
>
> *Buddha*

CHAPTER 20

Acceptance at Long Last

March 2013

I have learned through my journey back to me that conflict and confrontation can bring with them a deeper understanding of all around me; it does not have to bring war on my outside.

Jewish communities who come together yearly to mourn the Holocaust always say, "People like you and me did this—look no further." A prisoner has been heard to say, "People on the outside need us here on the inside to point their finger and say, 'They are bad,' so that they can feel better or good about themselves."

I know that good and bad are not always just on my outside; they are very much on my inside, and this is where I can start if I really want change for the better. I know now that we are all capable of good and bad in our mind, and when we lose control of our mind, we are capable of causing harm on the outside; and it is this very admission that is my salvation.

In the past when someone thought it okay to destroy my world, every fiber of my being cried revenge. Hatred consumed me; it took my sanity from within. But this sensation of being (and acting) out of control in reality only caused me to hate myself even more, thereby continuing the cycle of self-destruction. Hating myself (along with others for allowing them to do what they did to me in childhood) only served to kill my self-esteem—I felt and thought I was bad; therefore, I kept acting badly.

As I look back now, I am grateful that I somehow managed to contain my anger (all twenty-three years of it!) enough to just send texts to my family members. It took all of my power at the time of my emotional release to not go further—equal in my mind to the level of damage my family had bestowed upon me—possibly even as far as wanting to physically harm them. I wanted my family to feel the depth of pain that I had felt all these years from their ongoing nonaction and subsequent denial. This was to be my revenge.

The reality, though, was that I kept going to the wrong place for help, for help is a gift, a very precious one, and so it cannot be taken; it has to be given. I gravely underestimated my family's pain; they were unable to help, for their hearts too were in trauma. Such was the impact of alcoholism on every single one of us, including my dad. The "fuzziness" inside my mind had blinded me up to now, but the subsequent revealing truths of all helped me view everything from a fresh and clear perspective.

So now that I accept that the greatest battle I have is from within; nothing on the outside impacts me—only if I let it.

I have learned the art of this battle. It is called self-restraint and personal choice, and with my self-esteem back intact, I can be confident about making the right personal choices for me going forward. It was a lack of self-esteem that stopped me from taking appropriate action before now. I did not believe in me. I did not see my own power.

I know now that my power lies in personal choice. For I have the choice to generally accept healthy situations only and the choice to confront and try to influence change in unhealthy situations. And if I can't influence change, then the choice is to remove myself first physically and then mentally over time through a process of detachment with love and understanding.

I now choose to remove myself from unhealthy situations in the full awareness that it is not personal to me. Instead I take the situation personally and with it exercise whatever choice I deem necessary to protect myself from harm, including one-off dangerous situations or ongoing negativity.

Enacting my right to personal choice in a loving and kind manner is to me the essence of true love. True love to me is now about awareness and respect for our own and other people's boundaries— even in the absence of clear boundaries being set by others, as it is for us to set our own boundaries and live up to them regardless of circumstance. And without the motivation to overstep boundaries, I know now that there is no need for self-destructive emotions within me as there is simply no reason for them.

Instead the main focus of all my decisions is on a shared happy destiny with others, each deserving of their own, for I assume now that others are on the same path as me, just perhaps they are going along it a different way (through the enactment of their human right to personal choice). As a result, my new competitive spirit, my fight for a better life, now comes from deep within. It emanates from my life's purpose, and it is for me to join forces with it and with like-minded friends to drive change for the better of future generations.

I now hold in my heart and head all that I need to be free to be truly happy. And when I give myself permission to be happy, I know that I am following my destiny, for what use is a destiny if it is not a happy one? I no longer need to be motivated by guilt or an unheard anger; I can choose instead to be motivated by a deep acceptance that

I deserve to be happy and at peace in every little way, and all I have to do to make this happen is to take complete ownership for all the personal choices I make—aware and at times unaware.

This had been my true journey into adulthood. My world on the outside can now reflect all the choices I make on my inside. My inside and outside are at last at one. I am now truly in control. I am "master of my fate, captain of my soul."

In childhood I was repeatedly raped in every possible way, and my subsequent feelings and human need for justice and equality were ignored in favor of false harmony—my own as much as others. I was unsure of what to do or how to go about seeking justice or even knowing what justice and equality looked like. But now, after deep reflection, I have a clearer understanding of what justice and equality look like. I now want this to be a central part of my destiny going forward.

I believe that there are lessons here in my story to be learned. One of the key lessons I have personally learned is that all children deserve their voice to be heard equally against all others, particularly those who are much older. It is for us adults and parents to give our children the platform from which their voice can be heard. To me this means allowing our children freedom of expression in all ways productive to building their own self-esteem so that they can communicate their own life purpose.

I didn't get time in my youth to think through what I wanted to do with my life; I was simply too busy surviving one emotional trauma after the next. I didn't get time to explore my talents and skills and choose the right path in life for me and me alone—until now. Everything up to this point was accidental as I floated from one thing to the next without solid foundations; it certainly was not with a clear vision or sense of purpose.

*   *   *

Once I followed only what others said and what others did. I did not believe in me. I leave that part of my life behind me now—as

I no longer need to wait for someone else's permission to be happy with the choices I make that are right for me.

Now I stand ready by my truth. I do so not to make anyone else feel bad as I forgive all, including myself, for all past actions, for I believe that it was a lack of awareness that made us all do what we did—it has just taken me a long time to truly accept this very thing.

I also forgive the subsequent regret at being made aware of our unacceptable behavior, for this emotion too has prevented remedial action, and in a world where time is precious, this is such a waste of time. Regret, like anger, hate, or pain, only serves to keep us locked in our very own cycle of self-destruction.

I stand ready by my truth so that in the freedom of my written word I have gained peace of mind. The truth has set me free. It is my eternal hope that someday it will set all free too.

I now know we can only steer our destiny
from a place of neutrality—the whole truth—
thus making room for clear direction.
Otherwise we drift back and forth and around in circles.
Whatever our choice, and it is our choice, it
is legacy we leave to our children.

*   *   *

In early September 2012 I texted my sister Liz, giving her kind notice that the police would be contacting her and our sister Angela for a statement in relation to my final stand for justice against my one living abuser, Jonathon. She never replied to let me know that she got my text or notice.

In early November 2012 I texted my sister Liz saying that I would love to know what she and Angela said in her statement and that if she could let me know I would appreciate it. She never replied to my text.

In late November 2012, Pierce once again, of his own volition, made contact with Liz. Pierce laid out the facts—not the emotions—of my case to date as clearly and as calmly as he could. His feedback was that Liz was still hurting, and because of the depth of her pain she seemed unable to comprehend or deal with my pain. She also appeared to be dreading how this situation, if made public, would impact her and the broader family. There was little sign of my pain (the primary pain) being given priority.

On the upside, Pierce did through the course of their meeting finally gather information as to what exactly Liz and Angela did say to the police in support of my legal action against Jonathon. I had known that Liz's respectable standing in society wouldn't allow her not to tell Pierce what she said.

Liz and Angela had given a statement to the effect that they could not remember my mentioning Jonathon's name on the particular day in question, but nonetheless they wanted to assure the police (just not me either in person or via text/letter/e-mail or a call to Pierce) that they were supporting my statement in any other way possible for they were sure that if I was claiming now in front of the whole world that I said it, then I must have said it.

Shortly after this, my sister Liz tried to commit suicide. Thankfully she survived.

Thereafter, the police submitted my file to the DPP, the Irish state prosecutor. I have not heard back as to the outcome. I do not expect the state will bring my case to court, as I have no other evidence aside from circumstantial. My opening up to my sisters is classified as circumstantial along with evidence as to my mental state at the time—anorexia, suicidal tendencies, etc. For all of this, I would need my sisters' support (I know that my mum, because of her particular addictions, will never remember anything of my childhood).

Jonathon has been made aware of my statement and in response has categorically declined my allegation. Jonathon's wife was approached by the police and told of the details of my statement. As of yet, she remains in her marriage with two children.

I do still have an option to bring Jonathon to court on my own behalf. I am considering this.

There remains no contact between my family and me.

I quietly stand here by my truth. I patiently await my justice—fair and reasonable treatment—that I deserve and that only comes to those who dare to question. I know that day is now—in my writings—as you read this.

From the bottom of my heart, thank you for reading my story.

My memories are eternally mine; I choose now to allow room for beautiful ones. They are what magical dreams are made of. This is my fresh start.

> *I have a dream. In my dream my family and all families impacted by addiction tear down the walls of denial and come together united in their grief. In doing so, they acknowledge all that they too have lost. I dream that we all learn to understand about our childhood of neglect so as to learn how to change its impact on our children and us. I dream that we understand the need to seek external help, the need to read to gain more knowledge so that our children and we can have a better future, so that we all can have a better future.*

I have also been shown children of the future being
what the children of the past and the present have
not allowed be—real children full of wonder.

Lorna Byrne
Stairways to Heaven

To my family:

I am truly sorry for the pain I have so obviously caused you, knowing now as I do that all I was doing was triggering your own pain in you. I hope someday you will find it in your hearts to forgive me.

For my part I have learned such valuable lessons, lessons I would not have learned if I had gone any other way on my journey but this one, and for that I am eternally grateful.

I realize now that I was enabling you all to treat me the way you were treating me. By fighting with you I was trying earnestly to stay in the relationship; I was trying to change you in order to be able to do so.

Only in leaving you did I regain my dignity and self-respect. Only then did you truly get the message as it was intended in the first instance—that what you did and are continuing to do to me is unacceptable to me.

I realize now that I need to make my messages clearer going forward. Conflict is good if it leads to resolution, but both parties have to truly want to make it work. If one is unable to see the other side, in the longer term, then it is best to stand back and see what is best for all concerned. Sometimes that may mean having to leave your loved ones behind, and that is what I have chosen to do.

I realize now that children of childhood neglect do not want to question, as they do not want to think. This is the most natural thing in the world. It is one of the most effective survival mechanisms we have. It is not for me to tear those walls of yours down. It is for you to do it whenever you are ready.

I guess what was a surprise to me was your lack of sympathy, but I see that your own surprise was in my airing of my past at all. You saw no logic to it. You saw no reason, and that is where we differed—I saw every reason, and I was trying to instill this in you all too.

I have learned a lot about change in this process. I have learned that it is almost always unexpected and therefore devastating to start, especially if it is not handled with care and thought. I understand that was my flaw—not to have dealt with this change of mine in a more caring and thoughtful manner.

I realize now that I was willing to move through the change process more quickly than you, as I knew what was up ahead—I had a clear vision of a new me. I see that you didn't and still don't have that same vision, and without this vision, there is little motivation. I hope that someday upon reading this you will have motivation, not for me but for you.

I love you always. I am truly grateful for the hidden blessing you have bestowed upon me. I have become a much better, stronger person. I wish you all the freedom and happiness the world can bestow upon you.

6846673R00134

Printed in Great Britain
by Amazon.co.uk, Ltd.,
Marston Gate.